GEORGIE CLARK

GEORGIE CLARK

Thirty Years of River Running

by Georgie White Clark and Duane Newcomb

Chronicle Books San Francisco

Photo credits:
Joseph Muench, page 10, 11, 12, 21, 30, 38, 47, 50 top right, 57, 68, 80,
86, 99, 103, 106
William Belknap, Jr., page 37
Freda D. Walbrecht, page 49
B. Stackhouse, page 50, 52, 62, 77

Library of Congress Cataloging in Publication Data

Clark, Georgie White.
    Georgie Clark: thirty years of river running.

    Bibliography: p.
    1. Clark, Georgie White.   2. The West—Biography.
3. Rafting (Sports)—The West.   I. Newcomb, Duane G.,
joint author.   II. Title.
CT275.C6265A34   917.8′04′30924 [B]   77-25448
ISBN 0-87701-105-2

Design by Brenn Lea Pearson.
Cover photograph by Roy Shigley.
Composition by Hansen & Associates.
Printing by Fremont Litho.

Georgie Clark's long and successful career as a white water expedition leader has allowed her to share her thirst for adventure with thousands of brand-new river rats. How did a woman like Georgie find her way from the Midwest to the helm of her raft, and end up dripping wet and grinning from ear to ear? How did she begin to lead river parties deep into canyons and dense jungle in search of the best rapids?

Georgie shares many secrets in this exciting book, including her tricks for conquering the big spills that life sometimes provides. She has a sure way of taking control of the situation—even when it's her own sorrow—and turning it into a strength. GEORGIE CLARK is the life story of a brave and amusing woman whose adventures read like a race downstream.

Contents

Georgie – Woman of the River

Somewhere in the distance, I could hear the rapid as we floated past immense boulders, tiny in contrast to the sheer walls of the Grand Canyon towering hundreds of feet above us on either side. The roar was gradual at first, then grew louder and more ominous until suddenly, thundering like a freight train, the wild, vengeful river swept us twisting and turning toward a giant churning hole. I waited expectantly. The nose of the boat shot up. I clicked off the motor. The boat dove nose first into a twenty-foot hole, turned upward, then slammed sickeningly into a huge wave. The water soared over my head, soaking me to the skin, and I hung on for dear life to keep from being flipped backwards out of the boat. I waited. We burst through the wave on the other side. I hit the button. The motor roared. We shot through the rapid, then pulled into the rocks below to watch the little boats come through behind us.

The rapid we had just conquered was Lava Falls, the most feared rapid on the river. Years ago lava flowing down the side of a huge cinder cone here created a five-hundred-foot-high lava dam across the river. Over the years the water has worn down the lava, leaving what amounts to a roaring waterfall pouring over a series of hard lava boulders. The water at Lava leaps and gushes in snarling defiance, creating the most vicious, seathing hole to be found almost anywhere in the world. Lava Falls, has a ferocious reputation among river runners, and practically everyone of them has a Lava Falls horror story to tell.

My river flotilla, for running this and other rapids, this trip consisted of my "big boat," a thirty-five-foot neoprene raft lashed together with two twenty-seven-foot rafts, and the "thrill boat," three smaller neoprene rafts lashed together to make one boat.

I pulled in directly below the rapid to let the "river rats" on my boat scramble back over the rocks to watch the thrill boat come through. The front raft hit a wave, tilted crazily, balanced for a minute as if it were going over, then fell back in the water and went plunging through the raging rapid. In a few minutes they were pulled in beside us.

Five days before, this group of forty (ranging in age from five to eighty) running the river with me, had trouped off the bus at Lee's Ferry, Arizona to join me for this three-hundred-thirty-mile, ten-day Colorado River trip. Some were experienced river rats, others were completely green. All, however, had accumulated more white-water river experience than most Americans. In five more days we would take the rafts out at Temple Bar, Lake Mead.

In between Lee's Ferry and Temple Bar this group would plunge through the depths of the Grand Canyon to run over a hundred of the roughest rapids to be found anywhere in the world—rapids with such picturesque names as Sockdolager, Grapevine, Horn, and Little Bastard. During what was left of the summer I would

repeat this trip two more times before heading for Mexico for a river exploration trip there.

This is a typical summer in my life, for I am Georgie Clark, "Woman of the River," and I have made this white water trip through the Grand Canyon of the Colorado River more times than anyone else in the world, living or dead. In addition, I have pioneered more white water rivers in Mexico, Central America, South America, Canada and Alaska than any other American.

I know that it seems unusual that a woman has been pioneering the wild rivers of the world longer and with more success than most men, but I knew from the first moment I swam the Colorado River over thirty years ago that I had discovered the one great love of my life.

From then on I was determined to conquer the rapids. To accomplish this, of course, required great changes in methods, equipment and skills. But over the years, despite what, at times, seemed like insurmountable odds, my effort paid off. Today almost anyone of any age can run the roughest rapids. The river runners taking this trip with me are a good example of what I'm talking about when I make this statement.

River adventurers are expected to be rough and tough, right? Well, some of them are, but one of my most enthusiastic river rats this trip is six-year-old Sissy, a friendly, blue-eyed girl from Chicago running the river with her parents. Once we pull in at night Sissy looks at me to make sure it is okay, then jumps feet first off my raft into the river. Two nights ago I looked up to see Sissy hit one of my big

When this three-boat innovation of mine first appeared on the river it helped convince some of the old-timers that I was truly out of my mind.

brassiere and said, "You're not the only one who can wear one of these." As I looked closer I saw that it held his hearing aid so that it wouldn't get bounced out in the water. Back home in Iowa no one believes Willie runs rapids. So this summer he has insisted that we take a lot of movies of him so everyone will know the real truth.

Or take Kathy, a pretty, intelligent eight-year-old sent on this trip alone by her parents. The second night out, I discovered Kathy reading a letter from a boy back home. "Boys are such silly things, Georgie," she told me. "He can't even spell. I'm going to correct this letter and send it back."

I tried to tell her that she would be a lot happier if she just let it go. After all, what boy wants to get a letter back from his girl with the spelling corrected? I'm afraid, however, that it will take a few more years before she understands what I am talking about.

Or Bernice, a chunky, overweight, fifty-five-year-old bleached blonde who wears big floppy hats on the river. The second night out I heard this tap-tap, an unnatural sound for the river. I looked up and there was Bernice typing. She confided to me that she had brought along a mini-ature portable typewriter to take notes. What a character. At first I decided she was an aging movie actress. Then I dis-covered she worked in a Los Angeles fish market and sold magazine articles on the side. Bernice never rented a motel room like the rest of us. She was always short of money so she just threw her sleeping bag down in some out of the way place then joined us the next morning. In addition to

six-foot boatmen in the middle of the back with a mud ball. Darting after the giggling girl he grabbed her with one arm and smeared mud on her arms and legs. He thought that would stop her, but Sissy just picked up a handful of mud and threw it into his face. The last I saw of them, they were racing into the water laughing.

In addition to Sissy, I also have Willie, a spunky seventy-six-year-old who looks like the sort of person you might expect to find playing checkers in an old folks home. The first night on the river Willie came up to me, pulled up his shirt to expose a

This is Catarac Canyon, long famous for the Big Drop—fifteen miles of incredible rapids. Now, because of Glen Canyon Dam, the river is very calm and mild here.

the adventurous type, these are river rats who come on my trips.

White water river running is my life; I began here on the Colorado River by swimming the river, not once, but twice. I spent the next ten years trying to conquer the rapids in a ten-man raft. Finally I developed the equipment that allowed me to run all rapids easily. Up to the time I developed what I call the three-boat (or thrill boat), white water adventure attracted only a few die-hard enthusiasts. But from 1954 until the present, the interest in the sport has literally exploded.

I, of course, don't take all the credit for the present white water popularity, but many of the methods I pioneered on those early Colorado River trips are being used today by river runners everywhere. In addition, many of the television shorts, movies, and magazine pictures of rapid running in the 50s, 60s and even today were taken of my boats running the river.

So I like to think that I have played my part in creating today's tremendous white water popularity and in opening America's wild rivers to everyone, everywhere.

The Making of a White Water Adventurer

After thirty years of running rapids in both North and South America I guess it is safe to say that I have had more white water experience than anyone else in the world. In the beginning, of course, I wasn't trying to set any records, yet over the years, somehow, I've chalked up a long list of white water firsts.

At the time I became interested in the Colorado River in 1945, almost nobody was running the rapids there. A man named Norman Nevills was taking people through the Grand Canyon in wooden boats on a regular basis, but beyond that only a few adventurers braved the depths of the inner canyon.

When I swam the rapids of the Colorado River in a life jacket, first in 1945, then again in 1946, I was the first person (along with a companion) to attempt this feat. When I lashed three rafts together in 1954 and began to run rapids instead of portaging or lining through, I became the first river adventurer to run all rapids consistently. When I developed the Big G-boat in 1955 I became the first person to take large groups down the river.

My 1955 trip of 28 people marked a historic first. On that trip I took the largest single group downriver to ever go through the Grand Canyon at any one time. After all, from the time John Wesley Powell made his historic Grand Canyon trip in 1869, until 1955, fewer than 300 people had gone through the canyon. After 1955, for several years, every time I took a group through the canyon I set a new record.

When I flew to Mexico in 1958 to run the Rio Grande de Santiago, I became the first wilderness river runner to attempt any Mexican rapids. After that in rapid succession I chalked up firsts on the Balasas, the Grijalva and the Usumacinto, that runs along the border of Guatamala and Mexico.

When we tackled that portion of the Grijalva River the Mexicans call the Canyon of El Sumidero, we created a tremendous sensation. A number of people had attempted to run this river before but no one had succeeded. The summer before we ran El Sumidero, a Mexican army charting expedition had to be rescued by helicopter, and two months before we completed the trip successfully, a Spanish explorer disappeared in the canyon. Our small group, however, managed to portage and run the rapids here with only a minimum of difficulty.

Much to my surprise, when I decided to explore the North Country rivers in 1962, nobody had tackled any but the most accessible. In short order I racked up firsts on the Copper River, Alaska; the Nahanni, Northwest Territories; and the Big Bend of the Columbia, British Columbia.

On the Fraser River in British Columbia I created a turmoil. Four river explorers, some forty years before, had run the treacherous Hell's Gate Rapid and

lived. But nobody had tried it in recent years. I ran this rapid easily with thirteen men and women. The headlines in Vancouver proclaimed our feat and the two Canadians who went with us became instant local heroes.

I am sure that all of this makes me sound like some sort of super adventurer like the ones you read about who spend months hacking through the teeming jungles of South America, or who have their feet frozen off while climbing the world's highest mountains.

In a way I suppose tackling the wild untamed rivers of the world is true adventure in its own right, but I certainly don't live up to the image most people have of this type of person. I stand five feet, five inches tall, seldom weigh over one-hundred-thirty pounds, and look like somebody's secretary. As a result, in the early days I constantly startled people who knew of my reputation as a white water adventurer but who had never met me. Several times I've had people say, "You can't be a river explorer; you just don't look rugged enough." In my case I don't think running wild rivers had anything to do with size or strength.

From the moment I laid eyes on the Colorado River I loved the raging water and within a short time I realized that I was going to dedicate my life to this river and others like it. In many ways I am a fatalist about life, and while I'm not really religious, I do believe that whatever happens in life is preordained.

The reason why river running quickly became an obsession for me, I believe, lies deep in my background. And while I have done many different things during my lifetime and had many different experiences, they all seemed to have pointed me more or less in the same direction.

*   *   *

My roots in Chicago go very deep. I can't say that life was easy for me there during those first two-and-a-half decades of the 1900s, because it wasn't. My family lived for awhile in a rear basement flat of a tenement building joined to the other buildings on the block with a narrow side archway. Then we moved to a rundown brownstone in the same neighborhood. After that we lived in a number of similar buildings in the same area. At no time did we have a bathroom in our apartment. I well-remember having to stand in line almost every morning to use the bathroom down the hall. All the apartments at that time had a little window cooler instead of a refrigerator. Something was always wrong with the central heating and in the winter we were often cold. Besides this, our apartment had a hole in the wall through which we could see everything that went on next door. I didn't think very much of any of this at the time. I knew from my mother Tamor De Ross that life was supposed to be serious business and I just accepted it that way.

Looking back, I don't seem to have many memories of my father George De Ross. I know he had black curly hair and dark eyes. He also had a military bearing and could charm the spots off the walls. He talked himself into and out of a number of good jobs in those days including one as superintendent of a mine in a small community near Chicago. My father, however, should never have been married because he could never seem to accept the responsibility of a family. He would leave us in Chicago for months at a time and never send us a penny to live on. As a result, my mother soon had to support our family which at that time consisted of myself, my brother Paul (two years older than I) and Marie (seven years my senior).

Mother was the exact opposite of my father. She was hard working, dependable and industrious. When she realized that my father wasn't going to support the family she started looking for a job. Nobody wanted to hire a woman in those days so it took awhile before she finally found work in a commercial laundry.

My mother really had a way with women's clothes. If working conditions were the same then as they are now, I'm sure that she would have become a women's clothing designer or at the very least a custom seamstress. In Chicago during the early 1900s however, the closest she could come to that was to find a job ironing other people's clothes. I well-remember that mother would come home dead tired after a grueling day at the laundry, fix our dinner, then start scrubbing floors. Mother would never let us help with any of the chores because she always said she wanted us to have a pleasant childhood. After she finished cleaning our apartment to her satisfaction she would wash and iron our clothes and get the three of us ready for school the next day. Marie and I never owned more than one or two dresses at any time so this cleaning and ironing was always a nightly task.

Despite the fact that neither my sister nor I had many dresses, we were always the best dressed girls in school. Mother's sisters had married well-to-do men and her sisters always gave us their hand-me-downs which were always made of the very best material. Mother made these cast-off dresses over into some of the snappiest, best designed clothes I've ever seen. She refused to pay any attention to the fashion of the day but designed these dresses to look good on us. For instance, most women at that time were wearing long dresses but Marie was tall and looked much better in short dresses. As a result that's what mother insisted on making for her.

My mother, I believe, was years ahead of her time and although some psychologists would say she was repressive in many ways, actually, she left me with a number of traits that have proved extremely useful in later life. The first of these grew out of mother's insistence that I never cry or feel sorry for myself. I remember one time a boy knocked me down in the street and I came in with tears pouring down my cheeks. "Don't cry, Georgie," she told me. "If you cry every time something like this happens, you'll cry your life away. You must learn to accept life as it is."

At other times she would tell me not to cry because I had good health and good teeth and everything had to be up from there. After that if I felt like breaking into tears I would hide it from mother. In later years this admonition of mother's often helped me to go on when I felt down or discouraged.

Of course mother never asked us to

accept something she herself wouldn't put into practice. In her later years mother had an automobile accident that paralyzed her and put her in a wheelchair. I never heard one word of complaint. Despite her difficulties she insisted on scrubbing floors, fixing meals and running her treadle sewing machine with her one good leg (all from a wheelchair). Mother kept up this spirit right to the end. After she had been sent home from the hospital to die, she called me in one night and said, "Georgie, I must be two people, it's taking me so long to stop living."

Besides this attitude, mother passed on a calmness to me that has been useful throughout my life. She had the ability to stay calm and to act intelligently even in extreme emergency. While I don't think you can teach this to anyone, her example seems to have become deeply ingrained in my own personality. In an extreme emergency I find that thoughts of my mother's calmness come to me and I act out of reason instead of panic. One time on the river a propane stove somehow threw flaming fuel all over a nylon jumpsuit I was wearing. I yelled for the others standing around to put a blanket over me but no one moved. Finally, I rolled in the sand and put the flames out myself.

Another time in Mexico, by staying calm, I managed to save the lives of everyone with me, but that's a story for later in this book. It is enough to say here that however I acquired this calmness from mother I certainly want to thank her for it.

Mother also, throughout her life, was extremely straightlaced about being honest. I don't think I ever knew her to tell even a white lie. I remember one time

This is an aerial shot of the Rio Grande de Santiago where the rapids, even then, were waiting for me.

I promised to go on a date with a boy I really didn't care much about. When he called our house I asked mother to tell him I wasn't there.

"Don't you have any backbone, Georgie?" she asked me. "If you didn't want to go out with him you should have told him no when he asked the first time. As far as I am concerned if you are here, then you are here."

I'm not sure I have always been able to live up to mother's example, but I do think it would be tremendous if everyone believed and acted as she did.

Finally, mother had some influence on my becoming a vegetarian. She, of course, didn't cause me to become a vegetarian, but she always left me free to choose how I wanted to live. Most people become vegetarians in their later years because they feel they should eat vegetables instead of meat. That is not the way it happened to me. I simply haven't liked meat from childhood. Unfortunately, in our house, if you didn't eat what mother put on your plate you didn't get anything else in its place. So I wound up eating my vegetables and giving the rest to Paul and Marie. At that time the family had so little money coming in that we had meat for supper only about two times a week. Mostly I ate potatoes, cabbage, cole slaw, rice and tomatoes. We didn't have milk and I didn't like eggs. This diet, I found, gave me tremendous energy. When I hiked in my early days on the desert I often just took along some little cans of tomatoes. These sustained me quite well. Even today I consider tomatoes one of the staples of my diet.

In Chicago our house was only a few

blocks from Oak Street beach on Lake Michigan and that's where I got my first introduction to water. Right from the beginning I loved it, and every chance I got I headed for the lake.

At one time they put in some pilings near the Oak Street beach. The water would cover them completely, then it would go out leaving the tops of the pilings several feet above water, and then it would come back in again. The kids I hung around with at that time played games on these pilings. The one who could walk slowest and still avoid the water when it came in was undisputed leader.

One time five of us were playing this game on the pilings about three feet above the water. One freckle-faced kid managed to go slower than I could, then I tried to really slow down. Unfortunately I miscalculated. The water caught me and knocked me from piling to piling. When I crawled out shivering a couple of minutes later I was black-and-blue all over. Strangely enough, mother didn't say one word. This did, however, teach me a good lesson and after that I became extremely cautious around water.

Even after this catastrophe the beach and the water pulled me like a magnet. I was only about nine years old at the time but I decided I really needed to learn to swim. My mother couldn't afford lessons for me so I watched people swim and then tried to imitate them. My strokes, I am told, were far from perfect, but within a few months I could actually swim. I used to go from North Avenue—about a mile—to Oak Street in some of the roughest, coldest water I have ever known. I didn't know it at the time, but this was good

conditioning for the really cold water I encountered on many of the rivers I ran in later years.

Near Oak Street, at the Navy Pier, the Coast Guard kept several small boats which they used to run up and down the harbor. I hung around the pier for some time and soon became acquainted with all the young men running the boats. After a short time they made me their mascot and started inviting me aboard for short rides. That was my first experience with boats and I loved it. They soon began to let me steer and I would run up and down the wharfs with the Coast Guard sailors sitting in the front. I must say that those early years really sparked my interest in both boats and water.

The years after that all jumbled together in rapid succession for me. In my second year of high school I met and married a handsome, all American, six-foot, blonde young man by the name of Harold Clark. My mother had hoped that I would wait to get married until I finished high school. But she understood that I had strong sex needs and couldn't bring myself to fulfill them outside of marriage.

Young people today who find themselves in this situation simply live together. However, you just didn't do that when I was growing up. I know that I would have been better off if I could have defied convention. Outside of our sexual relationship Harold and I had nothing in common. In addition, I couldn't commit myself to Harold, or for that matter, any other man. Then at the age of seventeen, I gave birth to a daughter, Sommona Rose.

I had never been out of Chicago up to this time in my life and I was beginning to get restless. Young people today travel so much that they can't understand that people were so poor in those days that they neither traveled nor moved around much. I decided, however, that it was time I saw more of the country. I left Sommona Rose with my mother and my sister Marie and headed for Florida with Harold. We couldn't find work there, so we soon packed up and took the bus to New York City.

Once in New York I immediately began to look for work. At that time no one would hire a married woman so I told everyone that Harold was my brother. I answered every ad I could find for a week and by the end of that time, with the help of a stranger I met on a subway, I got a job as a Comptometer operator at Radio City.

Strangely enough even in those days I always seemed to find a job within a few days. They never paid much of a salary but we always ate. Harold, however, didn't find work the entire time we stayed in New York. Radio City is near Central Park and I used to walk over there on my days off to watch the six-day bicycle riders train. One day a couple of bicycle riders walked over to me and asked if I would like to learn to ride a bicycle. I was dubious at first, but interested. "Okay," I said.

Those were strange bicycles. They had very narrow saddle seats and no brakes. When you rode you strapped your feet to the peddles. I got the hang of keeping the bicycle upright in a short time, but I had trouble riding uphill. For awhile I was black-and-blue all over from falling on the uphill grades, but I finally mastered those

bicycles and rode all over Central Park.

Harold and I hiked a great deal around New York City and also swam in the oily water near the Queen Mary. I didn't care for either of these activities, however, and I kept asking the bicycle club members where I could get out in the country.

"You went the wrong way Georgie," they told me. "You should have gone to California."

Of course I could have gone to some other city in the East or the South, but California intrigued me.

"I'd like to go," I told them, "but I can't afford it. I just barely make enough to live on."

Well, surprisingly, the members got together and decided to give me one of their bicycles. I had never told them I had a husband so I said, "I'm afraid one bicycle won't be enough I have to take my brother with me." Surprisingly, they gave me another bicycle too.

That night I went back to our small apartment and told a startled Harold that we were headed for California.

"I'm going anyway," I told him. "You can come if you want to. If you don't want to go I'll leave you here."

Although I have been married most of my life, I'm afraid I've always been quite independent. I have always lived life my own way no matter what my husband thought. Of course that's not the way to get along with a man but then that is the way I have always been. Poor Harold. All he ever wanted to do was to settle down with a wife and live the rest of his life in one city. During the remainder of our marriage he was just never able to do this.

Then on Saturday, August 2, 1936, we left New York City, headed for California on two racer bicycles. Getting out of the city proved to be a problem. The bridge we crossed on—to this day I can't figure out which one it was—utilized the top level for cars and the bottom level for trucks. Naturally we started across with the cars, but before we had gone 500 feet a policeman stopped us and made us go down on the second level with the trucks. Peddling there proved terribly difficult because that lower level was paved with bricks. Unfortunately those bricks didn't stop at the end of the bridge either, but extended right on into the Allegheny Mountains. To top that off, the seat on that bicycle was so hard that by the end of the first day I had become so sore I couldn't sit down. In addition, I had pulled in behind a truck in the mountains, caught my tires in a track, and smashed my hand under the bicycle on the bricks. Tears came to my eyes, but I had learned mother's lesson well and I bit them back. I should have known that since I couldn't pull my fingers off the handle bars, I had broken my hand. But I had been taught from childhood to minimize the problems so I turned the handle bars up so I could grab them easily, poured turpentine on my hand and continued on toward Chicago.

By the time I reached Chicago I had bad blisters across much of my hand and a huge lump on my wrist. I rode over to the house of a doctor I knew, walked into his office and said, "I sprained my hand or something, would you look at it?"

He took one look and said, "Did you say sprain?" Then he took me into the inner office. "Georgie," he said, "your hand is broken. You have let it go so long, however, that I have to rebreak the big bone."

"No way am I going to sit around here while that bone heals," I told him. "I'm going to ride to California tomorrow."

"All right," he said, "but raise the handle bars again so that you don't put so much weight on your wrist."

The next morning we left Chicago headed down U.S. 66 toward California. From then on we averaged one hundred miles a day. About the fifth day out from Chicago I became extremely dusty and dirty and needed a bath in the worst way. Unfortunately, I had left New York with just one week's salary to take us all the way to California so I didn't have money for a luxury like a bath. I did know, however, that most rooming houses had bathrooms in the hall. So we rode into a small town in Missouri and I looked around until I spotted a big rooming house on a tree-lined street just a block from the main business district.

I must have had a tremendous amount of audacity in those days, for I simply walked into the hall, looked around until I found an open bathroom, walked in, locked the door and took a bath. When I finished my bath I put on clean clothes, opened the door and left. Over the next three weeks I repeated this performance at least twice in the small towns along the way, but I could never get Harold to try it.

We made excellent time all the way across Missouri, Oklahoma, and Texas. I guess there is no need to explain that we knew absolutely nothing about traveling cross-country by bicycle, because we rode the entire distance from New York to California without a spare tire or a patch kit. We also didn't own a sleeping bag. Every night we stopped out of sight somewhere near the highway and went to sleep. You could never do this safely today, but remember this was 1936. Outside the major cities most people were friendly and the countryside was reasonably safe. My hand had stopped hurting by this time, I had already gotten my bicycle legs, and I was really beginning to enjoy the trip.

I stopped at a bicycle shop somewhere along the way to have a chain tightened. The owner couldn't believe that we were riding across the country on those racing bicycles. They were only equipped with a high gear which meant we had to work extremely hard to pull any of the hills. He said, "I'm not going to let you go any farther until I fix those gears." Then he added a low gear so we could make the grades more easily. I had, however, become so used to peddling the hills in high gear that I never did use the extra gear the shop owner installed for us.

A few hundred miles after this we began to cross the western deserts. What a revelation that was! This was August, and the temperature soared into the low hundreds and the sweat poured off us as we peddled mile after mile across that open country. That desert seemed to stretch on endlessly and often it seemed to us that we could peddle an entire day without getting anywhere. I just couldn't believe that we could ride 100 to 125 miles without seeing at least one gas station. I was also so green in those days that I crossed the entire 800 miles of desert

without carrying a drop of water. Somehow we managed to peddle from one gas station to the next where we drank all the water we could swallow, then rested for a awhile in the shade beside the buildings. That terrific heat and the long ride were beginning to wear me down somewhat, but for the most part I was still in good spirits. Finally we came to a junction. The sign said: San Francisco one way—Los Angeles the other. What a sight that was! I hugged Harold with joy then we flipped a coin to decide which road to take. The coin came up Los Angeles so we peddled off in that direction.

Several days after that we arrived in Fontana, California. We now had exactly one dollar left. At that point I spotted a sign which read: *Grape Pickers Wanted.* Without hesitation we rode ten miles out to the ranch. The first question they asked was, did we have any experience? "Yes," I said, "we are very experienced."

That seemed good enough for them. They gave us a knife with a long blade and immediately put us to work. To make the day go faster Harold and I decided to see who could pick the most grapes. He picked fast, but he was too conscientious. I stuffed a lot of vines in the bottom of my basket and beat him, hands down.

At lunch the first day someone told me I could have all the wine I could drink. I hadn't eaten breakfast and I didn't have the money to buy sandwiches so I gulped down four glasses of wine in short order. Harold and I stayed with that job a couple of days, then we took the four dollars we had earned and peddled on toward Los Angeles. When we arrived we were almost broke. I went downtown immediately and

This is Marble Canyon where the red cliffs come alive in the springtime with yellow brittlebush and prickly pear cactus.

pawned a ring for seventy-five dollars so we would have enough money to eat while we looked for jobs.

That trip from New York to Los Angeles actually marked one of the turning points of my life. When I wanted to come to California I didn't ask how far or how hard the trip would be; I just came. Later, on the river I would learn to apply this principle to many of the difficult tasks I wanted to accomplish. When I wanted to find a way to run all the rapids without portaging, for instance, I didn't ask how hard the job would be, I just kept at it until I found a way. As a result, this trip provided me with a valuable lesson that I have utilized many times since.

Once in Los Angeles, I had to find a job. As usual, I went to work within a week. My first job turned out to be with a horse racing bookie. I don't remember how I found that job or why I took it, except that I needed money immediately. My job was to write the race results on the board. I worked there about six weeks, then quit.

"I like the job," I told my boss, "but they are closing these places left and right. As far as I can see nobody is going to put up bail to get me out of jail." Sure enough, two weeks after I quit, the police locked the doors and arrested several of the workers.

After that I managed to find a Comptometer job. During this time my brother Paul, my sister Marie and my mother joined me in California bringing Sommona Rose, who was eight by then. I was delighted to see them, especially my daughter. We had always been a close family even in the early Chicago days. Mother loved Los Angeles and I remember her

saying, "This is paradise. I'll never move back to the Midwest."

I had especially missed Marie. I call her my Rock of Gibraltar because she had always been there to back me up when I needed it.

Over the next few years I grew restless and moved from Los Angeles to Chicago and back several times. About this time Harold and I went our separate ways. Husbands have always come second with me. Harold just didn't want to move around like I did so we agreed to part. Later I filed for and obtained a divorce.

During the years I lived in Los Angeles I joined a small group of people who liked rock-climbing, hiking, ski-touring and bicycling. Outdoor sports weren't popular at that time and when cross-country skiing, for instance, we generally had the entire Sierra Nevada Mountains to ourselves. What a far cry from the conditions you find today! During that time I took many hikes in the Sierra and climbed many of the high desert peaks in Southern California. One of the people I frequently hiked with was a man by the name of Elgin Pierce. Later Elgin would become the first person to go through the Grand Canyon of the Colorado with me in a ten-man raft.

About this time I remarried. But, as I've mentioned before, I'm afraid I just wasn't meant for marriage. For awhile my new husband, James Whitey, tried to find a place in my life. He had some extreme personal problems which I agonized over, but eventually he went his way and I went mine.

World War II had now begun and I took a job on the security staff at Douglas

Aircraft. That triggered my interest in aviation. At that time the Ferry Command needed qualified women pilots to ferry planes within the United States. To qualify for this training I needed thirty-five hours of flying time. I quit Douglas, took all my savings out of the bank and began pilot training at Quartzsite, Arizona, the closest place where I could take flying lessons during the middle years of World War II.

When my daughter, Sommona Rose, and I arrived in Quartzsite I had just enough money left to feed us while I took flying lessons. I certainly didn't have enough left over to rent a place to stay. Sommona and I had by now hiked and camped together for several years in the California mountains. We simply threw our sleeping bags in a culvert next to the Quartzsite airport and stayed there for the next several weeks.

Sommona was a very mature thirteen by this time and the flight instructors loved her. Whenever they had time between students they took Sommona for rides and gave her free lessons. Actually, she learned to fly a lot quicker than I did.

When I finally soloed, Sommona came running out on the field as I touched down, climbed in and had me take her back up. When we came down a short time later, Sommona landed the plane. It was a far better landing than the one I had made earlier so for the rest of my flight training at Quartzsite, Sommona made the landings.

After I completed my required thirty-five hours of flying time, I applied for and was accepted into ferry pilot training at Sweetwater, Texas. By the time I completed my 500 hours of training, the war

This, on the left, is how I looked as a ferry command pilot at the end of World War II.

was nearing an end. The government deactivated the ferry command and sent me home to Los Angeles.

Sommona was now fifteen and had turned into an extremely attractive teenager. She had a great deal of artistic talent and was considering a career in commercial art. I, of course, had very little money, but one of her teachers had taken an interest in her and had arranged for a scholarship at a nearby college. The whole world seemed to lie just ahead. Sommona made it quite clear that she adored me. She also kept telling me that she had no intention of ever getting married, but I assumed that would change soon.

She and I went everywhere together. Sommona shared my love of the outdoors and we spent many weekends hiking and skiing. By this time she had already climbed most of the desert peaks in Southern California. She also helped me form a

This is my daughter, Sommona Rose, with me and our bicycling club in Los Angeles. Her death was the greatest tragedy of my life.

bicycle group we called the Hollywood Bicycle Club. In those days I couldn't interest many adults in bicycling but we did attract a number of seventeen- and eighteen-year-old boys. Almost every weekend we rode to Santa Barbara and back, a round trip distance of about 200 miles.

The last trip Sommona and I took together took place on a June weekend in 1944. We couldn't get anyone to ride with us that weekend so we struck off alone toward Santa Barbara. As we rode up the coast from Los Angeles we were serenaded by the waves of the Pacific Ocean pounding on the shore. I was happy that night and as we peddled along I could hear Sommona singing about fifteen feet in front of me. Suddenly, I heard the screech

of tires and almost without realizing it, I felt the ominous presence of a car bearing down on us from behind. It all happened so fast.

That car caught me, knocked me to the ground, and hit Sommona a solid, bone-crunching blow at the base of the brain with the rear-view mirror. Even before I came to a skidding stop on the pavement I knew Sommona was dead. She always called to me, "Georgie." This time, nothing. The car slowed, then stopped, and a man in a navy uniform stuck his head out the window. "Call an ambulance," I said. "I think she is dead."

I don't know how I knew he was going to run at that point, but I did. I can't even remember my own license number but somehow that night I had the presence of mind to memorize the license number of that car. Then with a squealing of tires he was gone.

In a few minutes a jeep came along and stopped. "Quick," I said, "take down this number before I forget it." Then I blurted out what happened.

Twenty minutes later the police and an ambulance arrived. I knew Sommona was dead but my mind wouldn't accept this, so I insisted they take her to the hospital first. As I knew, however, it was a futile gesture.

The next day the police traced the license number to a sailor about to be sent overseas by the navy. They wanted to know if I intended to press charges. I thought about it for a few minutes, then I said, "No, it won't bring her back."

I know this reaction will seem strange to some people. But I didn't want revenge. I just wanted my daughter back. For the next several weeks I couldn't think of anything but Sommona. I couldn't believe she was dead. My mind kept playing the death scene over and over and over. I stopped going out and stayed at home for the next several weeks. I just couldn't seem to snap out of my depression.

Then one afternoon some friends called. "Georgie," they said, "we're going to a party tonight. A man will be there to show color slides of the canyon country of Utah and Arizona. We're going to come by for you."

I started to protest, but they hung up before I could say anything. That night they picked me up at seven and took me out to Harry Aleson's house. I didn't know at the time that this was to be the start of a brand-new life. I was fascinated by the desert, the canyon walls and the huge rock formations.

Harry Aleson was a medium-sized man, probably twenty years older than I was, with graying hair and dark blue eyes. I told him that I would like to see the canyon country. And before I left we arranged to hike in the desert around the Grand Canyon. I had no idea that from this unobtrusive start I would wind up devoting my life to the wild rapids of the Colorado River. But then I guess many of the opportunities in our lives come to us by chance. All I can say is what I've mentioned before. I really believe that much of life is preordained. If I had not been at the right place at the right time in my life, I would have missed the fabulous adventure that was yet to come.

Surviving the Early Attempts on the Colorado

Within a few weeks after I met Harry and saw his pictures we began hiking together on the desert around the Colorado River. I have to say that it was love at first sight between myself and the Grand Canyon. I don't know what it was about that desert country and the river, but it felt right.

Harry, of course, had hiked along the Colorado River before, but in reality, we were both quite green in the ways of the desert. In the first place, neither of us knew the country well. I'm one of those people who don't like maps. I have never looked at one before going anywhere or carried one on a hike. Somehow I always have to learn about an area by experiencing it. In addition, I discovered that you can't trust the slate rock around the Grand Canyon. You think you have a firm footing, then suddenly the rock gives way. As a result you must learn to choose your hand and foot holds carefully and always to stay alert. The brittleness of this shale, I have discovered, causes many of the accidents and deaths among hikers along the canyon.

Harry and I really didn't know what kind of clothing or shoes to wear for desert travel. We also had no idea how much food we needed to carry for the number of days we intended to stay out. Somehow, despite these shortcomings we were always lucky. No matter what happened in those days we managed to overcome the problem. Sometimes our inexperience caused us extra work, but unlike a lot of desert hikers, neither Harry nor I ever had a serious accident.

Of course, I am a fatalist. I believe strongly that I will come through almost any experience without difficulty. And despite what have looked like overwhelming odds at times, this faith has always proved justified.

During the fall of 1944, Harry and I took a few preliminary hikes in the lower desert country around Lake Mead. Then Harry decided that along with Gerhard Bakker, a biologist from Los Angeles City College, we should hike from Quartermaster Canyon (where Harry had established a camp) to St. George, Utah, a hiking distance of about 125 miles. Along the route we would traverse some of the roughest desert mountain country in the United States. Starting at about 1100 feet on the river, we would climb out of the canyon, continue to rise across the desert plateau to above 5000 feet, then drop down into St. George, at an elevation of about 2800 feet. This was really quite an undertaking for three inexperienced people. Sometimes looking back, I wonder if we just didn't have dumb luck.

We left Boulder City, Nevada, August 13, 1944, crossed Lake Mead by power boat and proceeded from there up the Colorado River to Quartermaster Canyon. We then began our climb out to the canyon rim. At this point our inexperience began to show.

We hiked up Burnt Springs Canyon, then turned upward into Twin Springs Canyon. From the bottom Twin Springs Canyon had looked promising but as we neared the top we found ourselves cut off by two high cliffs. This is one of the things you really have to watch in the Grand Canyon. You just can't tell whether or not a canyon goes all the way to the top by looking. In later years, just to prove this to my river rats I used to ask them to pick the canyon they thought went to the top. Invariably, they would pick the largest side canyon they could find. Then to prove my point I would hike them up that canyon. Often it would end in a sheer wall before we had gone more than a mile.

By the time we reached the top of Twin Springs Canyon the two men were almost ready to collapse. I don't mean to imply that I don't get tired, but somehow, since Sommona occupied my mind completely at this point, I just didn't seem to feel anything at all. We now worked our way back to Burnt Canyon, then painfully followed that canyon to the top. The last several thousand feet I wasn't really sure Harry and Gerhard were going to make it. Besides being tired, their feet were killing them. They had worn narrow leather boots that rubbed badly. Every night after that they would take off their boots and together count their blisters. For desert hiking, that trip taught me, it is best to wear a type of shoe or boot with good ankle support but a canvas top.

At the top of Burnt Springs Canyon we headed roughly in the direction of St. George. At about this point, we believed, we were following the course of the two men who separated from the famous Major

John Wesley Powell Colorado River expedition of 1869 and were killed somewhere in the area. Powell, a veteran of Shiloh, led the first voyage to explore the Grand Canyon, the last unsurveyed and unexplored frontier in the United States.

Utilizing four custom boats designed to withstand the rapids, Powell entered the river at Green River, Utah, and after a hazardous trip of almost a thousand miles, he and his gaunt crew emerged into open country 65 miles from the settlement of Las Vegas, Nevada, August 29, 1869.

Gerhard, at this point, discovered a rattlesnake and insisted on capturing and carrying it with him on his back in a small muslin bag. From then on we shared all our water with that snake.

During the day's hiking the snake became accustomed to our movements and kept quiet. At night, however, that snake became supersensitive and every time I turned over it rattled. What an eerie noise that was.

I have been extremely sensitive to animals all my life. Even snakes, I feel, are part of nature and should be left in their natural environment. I couldn't make Gerhard put that snake back, but in my later trips on the river, over which I had complete control, I made sure that everyone with me left the animals completely alone.

We were now hiking in heavy timber on the Sheviwits Plateau south of St. George. This was the first hiking we had done here. We couldn't see any landmarks, and everything began to look alike. Finally Harry said to me, "Georgie I think we've been hiking in a big circle." Sure enough, when we checked we had almost come back to where we had started that morning.

Nothing like this has ever happened to me before or since, but in those days we were terribly unfamiliar with the desert country and simply had to learn by trial and error. After that, we watched the sun carefully to keep on course.

On the seventh day, somewhere out there on that desert, we met a hunter and trapper from Utah who offered us a ride to St. George. I didn't want anything to do with either him or his boys because I knew he was out there shooting wild horses. Harry and Gerhard, however, talked me into accepting the ride. I hated it. On the way back the boys spotted a beaver, stopped the truck, got out, and clubbed it to death. I know at that time a lot of people believed in killing animals. But I didn't. As far as I was concerned, that hunter and his boys were just not nice people, and I was relieved to leave them in St. George.

We had many hiking experiences in those days, some of them especially eventful because of our inexperience. On one hike, for instance, we drove into Marble Canyon near Lee's Ferry, Arizona, to hike to Little Nankaweep on the river. There was snow on the ground but we managed to reach the river easily without getting lost. Once down we turned around almost immediately and headed back toward the top. What a steep hike out that was! We both reached the top exhausted. When the truck came into sight, we heaved a sigh of relief and threw the packs in the back.

Harry crawled into the truck and stepped on the starter—nothing. Apparently, since we had driven out there in heavy fog, we had left the truck lights on and drained the battery. What a feeling! We were both tired and hungry. We certainly didn't want to hike anymore but we just didn't have a choice. Nobody used this road and we probably wouldn't get any help out here over the next three or four months. In addition we had finished our last bit of food back in the canyon. If we wanted to eat we had to get back to town. With those two thoughts in mind, we crawled out of the truck and started wearily back down the road to Buffalo Ranch, nineteen miles away. The State of Arizona maintained a large herd of buffalo here. At ranch headquarters they had built a residence for the ranch manager and several outbuildings.

The wind blew fiercely across the desert that night, making hiking difficult. In addition, every time we took a step we sank up to our ankles in sand. Almost exhausted we reached the ranch at four o'clock in the morning. The buildings looked completely deserted. I knocked on the door of the ranch manager's cabin, but no one answered.

Since we could do nothing more at that point, Harry and I sprawled out on the ground beside the cabin and went to sleep. At nine in the morning the ranger showed up. After listening to our problem he drove us, in his four-wheel-drive vehicle, back to our truck where we installed his spare battery and headed toward the highway.

Despite the occasional difficulties we ran into, those early hiking days were good ones for me. Much of the time right after my daughter's death I hardly knew where I was or what I was doing. Thoughts of Sommona completely occupied my mind. All I knew out there on those desert trails was that I had to keep putting one foot in front of the other. Strangely enough, no matter how difficult the hike in those days,

I never felt tired. That is when I realized that if you could control your mind you could make your body do anything. With my mind on Sommona's death, nothing else seemed to matter. I didn't care whether I got tired, ate food, or even lived or died. Looking back now, I know that the best thing I could have done at the time was to take those long hikes with Harry. While they did not take my mind off of Sommona, they acted as therapy to cleanse and renew me.

Harry, unfortunately, had his own problems. He had been gassed in World War I and it took a terrific toll. Most of the time he could hike without difficulty, but then the terrible stomach cramps would hit and he would roll on the ground with pain. It was a heart-rending sight. As a result, I never knew when Harry would get sick and we would have to lay over a day while he endured the pain. I lived constantly with the fear that he might die out there on the desert. If Harry became seriously ill I knew I could never hike several hundred miles for a doctor and return in time to help. Because of his stomach problem Harry ate nothing but baby food. A number of people poked fun at him, but he ignored all this. I had to admire Harry. He had more determination and sheer guts than anybody I knew. I had seen him hike for hours when I knew the pain was killing him. He had made a decision to explore the desert on foot and despite all obstacles he intended to do just that.

I knew that there were a lot of questions about my relationship with Harry. After all, I was married and spending weeks and months out on the desert with another man. The truth was that after seeing

This is the place I call home—the Colorado. This view is from Quartermaster in Lower Granite.

Harry's pictures I became determined to explore the desert and the canyon country for myself. I couldn't hike alone (at least I didn't think I could at the time) and Harry was the only person who would go with me.

After awhile I came to admire his drive and determination, but I was never romantically attracted to him, nor was our relationship physical. Harry simply needed someone to hike with him and be on hand in case of an emergency—so did I.

In those early hiking days Harry had a camp on the banks of the Colorado River at Quartermaster Canyon and every time we camped there we would drop into the water and swim short distances.

What an exhilarating feeling! I knew nothing about the deep canyon country, the sheer canyon walls, the turbulent water or the tremendous power of the rapids. Harry, however, had hiked some along the river and everytime he talked about the inner canyon I became more intrigued. First we talked about coming down the canyon in a boat and wondered if we could swim in our life preservers if we lost the boat. Unfortunately, neither Harry nor I could afford a raft. Finally Harry said to me, "Georgie, we will probably never run the canyon at this rate."

"Harry," I answered, "instead of waiting to save the money to buy a raft why don't we swim part of the lower canyon in our life preservers?"

Harry was reluctant at first, but after I talked about it several times, he finally agreed to swim the canyon with me that next spring.

That winter, Harry and I decided we would drive to Boulder City, Nevada and take a bus from there to Peach Springs, Arizona on U.S. 66. From there we would hike north about twenty miles across the desert to the river.

When we left Los Angeles that June we took the clothes on our backs, a life preserver and a malt can packed with pure sugar candy, powdered coffee and dehydrated soup. In those days, unfortunately, waterproof neoprene bags simply did not exist.

When we reached Peach Springs, we stripped down to swimsuits, tennis shoes, a shirt, a light jacket and a life preserver. We asked the sheriff to ship the rest of our clothes back to Boulder City so that we would have them when we came out. We then started toward the river. The heat radiating off the desert made hiking extremely difficult.

When we reached the river we stared in disbelief. The spring runoff that year was tremendous. The current hurtled at breakneck speed downriver, creating huge waves that crashed headlong into giant rocks. At the rapids the water roared across giant slablike rocks creating holes beyond that looked big enough to swallow a good-sized moving van. As if this wasn't enough, the spring rains had brought tremendous quantities of driftwood from the sidestreams into the Colorado River, creating a river of trees.

We had intended to swim awhile, then climb out whenever we felt tired, but the current was so strong that we immediately abandoned this idea and decided just to take our chances.

Harry waded in first. The current caught him from behind, knocked his hat into the water and carried him out of sight around the bend. I followed reluctantly. The current grabbed me and swept me downstream at breakneck speed. What a helpless feeling! As I shot along I had the feeling that I had passed Harry in the current, but I wasn't positive. Another ten minutes went by. The current swung me near shore. Here I managed to get into a backwater and work myself over to the bank. My breath was now coming in huge, gasping sobs. The struggle against the river had taken its toll, and I wearily inched myself up on the bank.

I couldn't see Harry anywhere. Had I dreamed I passed him in the water? I waited. I just knew he had drowned. Suddenly I heard a shout downstream. It was Harry. Slowly he worked his way upriver to where I was sitting. Apparently I had passed him, then he had repassed me in the water. He hadn't been able to climb out either until the river finally tossed him into a backwater. For almost twenty minutes after that, he lay there half in the water, half out, too tired to move. It was a terrifying experience. We both knew that somehow from then on we must stay together. For the next twenty minutes we worked to find a handgrip that could withstand the terrific force of the water. Finally we came up with a promising wristlock that looked like it might work.

"Shall we try it?" Harry asked.

I just nodded.

We stepped into the river then. The current caught us and shot us downstream. For the next six hours we careened through the rapids, fought giant waves and bounced around like two bobbing corks. It was like riding a roller coaster made of water. But the wrist grip really worked and we stayed

together as if locked in a vice. Time after time, Harry and I tried to make the bank, but the raging water kept forcing us downstream. By this point my body ached all over.

Then, suddenly, we rounded a bend and were sucked without warning into a black rotating whirlpool. In that water, passing at 125,000 cubic feet a second, those giant whirlpools had a life of their own. In the lower water of today there are a few miscellaneous whirlpools on the river, but nothing like the giants of that day. Round and round we went. All afternoon that wristlock worked well. But now it proved to be a terrible handicap. The whirlpool plunged me under head first dragging Harry feet first. Then it threw me out and pulled Harry under head first.

The first time I plunged into the hole time stood still, and my lungs began to burn. When I thought I couldn't hold my breath any longer I burst out, gulped for air and went under again.

This time my heart pounded in my ears. My chest felt like it was about to burst. Then the whirlpool shot me out again. I grasped for breath and struggled desperately to stay on top, but I couldn't fight that whirlpool and it pulled me under again. I knew that third time had to be the end. The pain was unbearable. I held my nose with my free hand and tried to hold off the inevitable. It was no use. I had to breathe. Suddenly everything turned topsy turvy. The whirlpool caught both of us and threw us violently against a rock wall. I grabbed the rock desperately and hung on. Whenever I tell people about this experience they always ask how long that whirlpool held me under. Actually I have no way of knowing, but it seemed like an eternity.

For a few minutes Harry and I just hung onto the rock and tried to catch our breath. The ferocious current sucked at our legs trying to pull us back in the water. We felt weak, drained and cold. I wasn't even sure I had the strength to pull myself up on that rock. Finally we inched out of the water and lay shivering on that narrow rock ledge.

It was now turning dark fast. I knew we couldn't get back in the river again because we had no way to know when we could crawl back out again. Besides that, I didn't even know that we could swim through the whirlpool. It had already sucked us down three times, but the truth was that we had to challenge it again if we intended to swim on down the river. With that thought we tried to settle down for the night. I wanted to build a fire, but even with a whole river of wood right at my fingertips, I couldn't fish out a single stick. Finally I gave up and mixed our coffee powder with the cold, muddy water from the river. It tasted terrible. Then we finished our supper by eating a few pieces of sugar candy. Finally I leaned back against the rock and tried to rest. Both Harry and I kept on the cold, wet life jackets because on that narrow rock ledge, we could easily tumble off into the water and get swept down the river.

All night long I kept wondering if we were going to die right there.

Finally light began to creep into the sky at the eastern end of the canyon. We drank some more cold coffee, ate a few more pieces of sugar candy and prepared to leave. The thought of that whirlpool hung heavy over us so we avoided looking at the river. Finally I said to Harry, "Are you ready?"

He looked at me and said, "I'm as ready as I will ever be." We joined hands in the wristlock and turned toward the whirlpool. For a full minute I just stared in amazement. There was no whirlpool.

The water still roared past at top speed, but that whirlpool had simply vanished in the night. Later I learned that this happens frequently on the river. A whirlpool will form right under you then travel to high water or disappear completely.

Harry and I swam the rest of the way to Lake Mead without real difficulty. Of course we still had trouble climbing out on the bank in that big, fast water. I had thought the logical place to land would be the beaches at the head of a rapid. I found, though, if I worked my way toward shore, yet missed landing, I would smash into the boulders at the head of the rapid. Finally I learned to land right in the middle of the fastest water. High waves impeded my progress, but I couldn't get cut on the rocks.

By this time we were starving. We had eaten almost nothing at this point except coffee, sugar candy and a little soup. Before the trip, however, Harry had come up by boat and cached food at Quartermaster Canyon. Now as we approached the food cache we intended to stop and eat our first real meal since we had started this swim.

When we approached the landing spot, Harry and I paddled furiously trying to work inshore. That was a futile effort. The raging current carried us right on past. About a mile downstream we managed to grab a rock and climb out. Now we had to

hike back. It was worth the effort, however, and to this day I'll never forget how
good that meal tasted.

On the third day, sixty miles below
where we entered the river, we reached the
backwater of Lake Mead. There we found a
several-mile-long log jam created by the
tremendous amounts of driftwood coming
down the river. I tried to push the trees
aside and swim through. I couldn't budge
them. I then tried to walk on top of the
logs. But they sunk under my weight.
Finally Harry and I climbed out on shore
and walked for miles around the edge.

Eventually the logs began to thin out.
We could swim again, but a strong head-
wind slowed our progress across the lake.
When I finally crawled out of the water at
Pierce's Ferry several hours later, my arms
and legs really ached.

Lake Mead is a typical large desert lake
surrounded by low, barren hills. Pierce's
Ferry, on the lakeshore, is an absolutely
desolate spot where a narrow dirt road
winds in from the main highway fifty
miles away.

At Pierce's Ferry we found one lone
man who had moved here from the east to
try to cure his tuberculosis. Outside of
him we didn't see another soul. Now we
had to hike that seventy miles across that
hot, dry June desert. It was a temptation to
sit and wait for somebody to come along
with a car. In those days you could easily
wait a month for anyone to drive into
Pierce's Ferry.

So, shrugging our shoulders, we trudged
off toward the highway. The trip took a
good three days and still left us seventy-
five miles away from Boulder City. At that

time you could flag a bus anywhere on the
highway, so we decided to wait for a Greyhound. We were, of course, still wearing
only bathing suits and light shirts. Harry
hadn't shaved for several days, and I hadn't
even tried to brush my hair.

I can just imagine the look on that bus
driver's face when he saw the two ragged
figures standing out there on that lonely
road trying to flag him down. But the bus
stopped and Harry and I crawled aboard
and reached Boulder City a few hours later.

The first month or so that I was back
in Los Angeles I couldn't possibly have
been talked into going for another swim on
the Colorado River. In the meantime Harry
and I started hiking again in the Grand
Canyon country. Over the next six months
we probably covered two or three hundred
miles looking at old mines and other
interesting areas we wanted to explore.

As time passed, both Harry and I began
to glorify the trip. Every time we mentioned it after that we forgot the pain and
remembered only the good parts. I was also
beginning to wonder what it would be like
to cover twice the distance we had swum
that first summer. After all, there was a lot
more river to explore up there in that
canyon. Finally I made up my mind that I
wanted to try swimming it again.

I knew I couldn't go alone, but I wasn't
sure Harry would agree to go with me.
Whenever we talked before he had been
quite firm about never going again. When I
brought the subject up this time he looked
like I had slapped him. "Are you crazy
Georgie?"

"Okay," I told him. "I'll go by myself. I
can find my way down to the river."

I could see that this got to him. So every time I saw Harry after that I began to tell him about my plans.

Finally he gave a long sigh, "Okay Georgie, you win. We'll try the river again."

Our next swim took place in the following June of 1946 at high water time. We drove to St. George and from there hiked the 120 miles to the river. Harry and I knew the desert country better than we had on previous trips, but we still didn't know it very well. We had stopped at a spring on our 1944 trip from the river to St. George, but somehow we missed it this time and drank every drop of water in our canteen.

The temperature soared to 120 degrees on the desert and we began to need water badly. At one point I noticed some swarming bees and on the chance that they were after water I started digging. About six inches below the surface I found a small amount of dirty water. After the bees took their turn we tried to drink some but found the taste almost unbearable.

I had also heard somewhere that cactus was a good source of water, so I cut one open and started to chew. I made a big mistake. It tasted like a mouthful of hemp and I spit it out immediately.

At this point we just headed in the direction of the river. We didn't get rimmed off and run into a dead end as many hikers do, but I fell several times on the shale trying to climb down over the cliffs, and ripped my bathing suit in several places.

When we reached the river early the fourth morning we found it a raging giant again and the driftwood poured past in an ever-present stream. I could hardly wait to start swimming this time. Harry and I locked our wrists together and stepped off the bank. The current caught us and shot us downstream toward some nearby rapids. Huge waves broke around us, but we just put our feet forward and bounced through the rapid without difficulty. A warm feeling of exhilaration swept through me. There was no doubt at all in my mind that the water was my friend.

Suddenly I was conscious of Harry coughing and coughing. In that rapid he had somehow taken a lot of water into his lungs. After a few minutes I managed to drag him ashore where he simply doubled up in pain. Fear swept through me. I really felt terrible. I had talked Harry into coming against his will. I wouldn't forgive myself if something happened to him.

After awhile, however, Harry got better and we were able to continue on downriver. I was now learning to relax and not to fear the rapids and the deep water.

At one point on that trip the river threw me against what I thought was a rock. I grabbed hold and pulled myself out. My rock I discovered was an old iron boat. Since that time I have tried to find out about the boat, but nobody seems to know anything about how it got there. It can still be seen today high up on the river bank, a reminder of the highwater days on the Colorado River.

By this time we were fast approaching Bridge Canyon Dam site. The Government was considering construction of a dam there that would back the water clear up into Grand Canyon National Park. They had established a rather elaborate camp on a long, narrow, flat spot about fifty feet above the river. We swept around the bend downstream and in the swift current passed directly below the camp. Suddenly the cooks spotted us, jumped up and ran to the edge of camp waving their arms. I guess they wanted us to stop. In that fast water, however, we couldn't even slow down. As we swept out of sight I could still see those cooks standing there dumbfounded trying to figure out what to do.

Shortly after this we began to notice planes circling the canyon. At first we didn't think it meant anything. Then we began to wonder if they were looking for us. Finally, Harry broke down and confessed that he had worried about swimming the canyon this year, so he mentioned it to some friends in Las Vegas. They in turn notified the newspaper.

Las Vegas was in desperate need of publicity in those days so someone released the story that we were behind schedule and must have drowned. Next, the newspaper headlines screamed: TWO DROWNED IN GRAND CANYON.

Back in Los Angeles the phone at my mother's house rang and the voice on the other end said: "We have the bodies of your daughter and her friend. Can you come downtown and identify them?" I don't know why people play pranks like this, but it seems to happen often in these cases. My mother had great faith in me, however, so she simply hung up and forgot the whole incident.

In the meantime we arrived at Lake Mead where a photographer and some publicists met us in a boat. Instead of giving us a friendly welcome, however, they accused us, rather vehemently, of being behind schedule. I had never promised anyone that I was going to come out of the canyon at any particular time, so I couldn't understand the fuss. Actually I had a feeling that they were peeved that we had showed up alive. After all they could have obtained a lot more publicity if we had drowned in the canyon.

Harry and I then returned to Los Angeles and within a few weeks most of the clamor died down.

That was the last time we swam the river in a life jacket. Harry told me if I wanted to go again I had to go alone. People often asked me how I could have done something so foolish. Actually those two swims proved invaluable. I learned more about water and the Colorado River on those two trips than I could probably have learned in ten years any other way. I came to understand how the currents acted both on and below the surface. I saw first hand how rocks affect the water and I learned some important lessons about controlling myself in high water.

I doubt very much that I would want to swim the river today unless I could go down in a wet suit. Since the Bureau of Reclamation built Glen Canyon Dam above Lee's Ferry, the water flowing through the Grand Canyon comes out of the bottom of the dam at a temperature of about fifty-five degrees Fahrenheit. This is much colder than the water I swam in during those early years.

The Park Service tries to discourage swimming today on the Colorado River. Every year people try it and drown. Just

Here I am with Harry Aleson at the end of the 125-mile Colorado River swim in 1946. The headlines said we had drowned but here we look pretty lively to me.

recently I picked up the air mattress of a young man who tried to cross the river at Phantom Ranch and just didn't make it.

Those early swims that I made on the Colorado River were probably some of the most exciting times of my life. After that when I finally started navigating the river in a ten-man raft it felt like the Queen Mary under me. Any raft, of course, no matter how small provided a lot more flotation than a life jacket. As a result of these swims, no matter what I encountered in later years, I really felt comfortable and at home on the water.

Pioneering the Colorado

*T*hose early life preserver trips on the Colorado River, far from discouraging me, just whetted my appetite for more river. It is true that my two swims during the summer of 1945 and 1946 were physically exhausting, but they were also exhilarating. Each time I shot lurching and twisting through a rapid with the water pounding me from every direction I had a deep welling feeling of excitement that I had never felt before.

I've had people tell me that an experience like that would absolutely terrify them. But after more than thirty years of river adventure I can only conclude that I am just not like other people, for I have never had any of those feelings. Every river experience I have had has always left me ready for the next adventure, and even after all these years I still can't get enough.

The Colorado River is a creature of change. In the early days the river would start out as a roaring giant of 125,000 cubic feet of water per second, then within the course of a week it would sometimes drop to almost a trickle. As I have discovered over the years, each rapid takes on an entirely different personality at different water levels. Hance Rapid, for instance, is barely a ripple in high water, but in low water it is a churning monster that commands everyone's respect.

I don't know what it is about the human mind, but somehow people like to number and label everything. So I guess it was inevitable that someone would develop a rating system for the Colorado River rapids which rates the rapids on a scale of zero to ten with the most difficult being a ten. As far as I am concerned, this rating system is nonsense. The difficulty of a rapid depends on the amount of water flowing through a rapid and the type of boat running through that rapid. I can, for instance, run some rapids very easily in my big boat that are extremely difficult to negotiate in a smaller boat. Some rapids are fierce in low water, almost non-existent in high water, and the reverse is also true. The amount of water flowing through a rapid varies every day. For instance I always try to run Lava the first thing in the morning when the water released from the Glen Canyon Dam reaches that rapid and makes it more interesting to run. Since this water from the dam reaches different rapids at different times, it means that the difficulty of a rapid to run will vary a great deal from hour to hour.

The Colorado River, I have found, is entirely different each time I run it. As a number of river runners have learned, to their regret, the river is always a challenge, one slip and it has you in trouble. This characteristic of the river, even today, satisfies my basic need for constant change and challenge. I have a strong feeling and a loyalty for the river that even I don't understand. When I'm asked about it I always say that I am married to the river

and I guess that is pretty close to the truth. Though I have never been able to commit myself to a man, that is exactly what I have done with the river.

*   *   *

At this point in my career, after having gone down the river twice in a life preserver, I wasn't at all adverse to running it again that way. I had learned a lot from that second swim and I think I could have learned even more from a third.

But Harry wouldn't hear of it. That second swim was still very fresh and very painful in his mind. He also remembered that I had intimidated him into going with me that second time. "Don't talk to me about swimming the river again, Georgie," he told me. "I won't listen."

Actually, I wasn't against keeping after him until he gave in, but I asked myself how I would feel if something happened. And I knew that I would never forgive myself if I were responsible for Harry being hurt or killed. That meant that if Harry and I were going to run the river together again that we would need a raft; the surplus kind were just coming on the market in 1946. After looking around the Los Angeles surplus stores for several weeks, I purchased a ten-man raft, and Harry bought a seven-man one.

There wasn't any doubt in our minds that we wanted to tackle the Colorado River again, the questions were: *where* and *how*? Neither of us now owned a car. Harry had sold his and I just didn't own one. I suppose that seems strange today. But in the 1940s money was tight for me. Also most of the time I just didn't need an automobile. As long as I stayed in the well-populated parts of the Los Angeles area I could easily get around on public transportation.

The lack of a car pretty well limited our access points to the river. If we took a bus from Los Angeles and hiked from Peach Springs, Arizona, as we had done the first time, it would mean carrying a 250-pound raft almost twenty miles. Coming in from St. George, Utah was also out of the question. We could launch at Lee's Ferry, Arizona, where all the Grand Canyon trips start today, but at that time there was no public transportation there. However, a Greyhound bus crossed the Green River just east of the town of Green River, Utah, and we could launch there, float Labyrinth and Stillwater Canyons of the Green River, join the Colorado River, run Catarac Canyon and take out at Hite, Utah, a total distance of about 150 miles.

Catarac, we felt, was an excellent choice. The canyon had a fifty-mile stretch of rapids probably second to none in the United States. In this area the river dropped 415 feet in fifty miles. It was like a mammoth roller coaster, a tremendous series of rapids that would thrill even the most jaded river runner.

Most river adventurers tackle a river during the summer months. After all, rapids themselves are enough of a challenge without taking on nature at her worst. At that time though, I was starting to sell real estate in Los Angeles. Since sales generally slowed down during the winter months, I decided this would be a good time to go.

I had never been out on the high desert of Utah, Arizona, or Nevada in winter and I had no idea what conditions we would encounter. Since the temperatures in Los Angeles during winter generally stay in the seventies and eighties it never occurred to me that it would be much different on the river. The truth was that November, the month we picked, could be miserable in the upper desert. Temperatures there frequently drop into the low twenties with driving winds and blowing snow.

November 12, 1946, I left Los Angeles by bus and met Harry in Richfield, Utah, where he was now staying. We then proceeded to board a bus for Green River. I can still see the look on that driver's face when he saw Harry's seven-man, 250-pound raft sitting there on the sidewalk.

"You can't take that," he told us.

"You don't have many passengers," I said. "You should have room for it in the baggage compartment." In the end he agreed to move some other baggage around and squeeze our raft in somehow. Harry and I then hurried aboard before he could change his mind.

Sometime later the bus dropped us off on Highway 50 just east of Green River. The highway here comes within a short distance of the river and offers easy access to the water. The minute we stepped off the bus that cold driving wind hit me right between the shoulder blades. The light jacket I was wearing did nothing to stop it and by the time we reached the river with the raft, my hands were shaking uncontrollably. I am not usually bothered by cold, but I certainly felt it on that trip. I'll never forget Harry scrunching up his shoulders, blowing on his hands and stomping around to keep warm. "Maybe we shouldn't try it, Georgie," he said. "We could go back."

"No way," I told him. "I've come this far. I'm going the rest of the way."

Rather reluctantly he helped me push the raft into the water and we were off on a five-day trip down the river. The current here was extremely swift. The first few miles the river ran through fairly open desert country, then just below the juncture with the San Rafael River, we entered Labyrinth Canyon. The scenery in this area and below in Stillwater Canyon was absolutely spectacular with views of giant red plateaus and mesas.

I'm afraid, however, I wasn't much in the mood to enjoy the scenery. The wind and the swirling snow made that part of the trip all but unbearable. It went on like this for three days. The water on the Green River was swift, but we didn't encounter any rapids.

Then about one hundred miles from the town of Green River, we joined the Colorado River and shortly afterwards entered Catarac Canyon. A few miles later we rounded a bend and shot almost without warning into our first rapid. Canyon walls here rose sheer on both sides and the water plunged through narrow fast chutes around huge midstream boulders. We shot suddenly through one of these chutes banging against the rocks as water pounded us from all sides. We were now literally bouncing from rock to rock. The raft suddenly flipped upside down and—with Harry and me hanging on—banged through the rest of the rapid.

Within a mile we managed to work our way ashore and climb out on a small ledge. Fingers of biting cold seemed to shoot all the way through my body. With shaking hands I gathered driftwood and managed to start a small fire. Even then, the stiff wind blowing upstream made it almost impossible to get warm.

Conditions on the river were bearable only when we kept moving; otherwise our arms and legs became extremely numb. We did stop every night but not because we wanted to. It would have been suicide to run the river after dark. Most nights we simply walked up and down to keep warm and greeted the first light of dawn with great relief. We could now start down the river again.

The next fifty miles were almost a repeat of that first rapid over and over again. We were now running what was known as the "Big Drop." The river was so low that all the rocks were exposed and the swift white water churned foam through the narrow chutes tossing our small raft around like a match box.

Some rapids we portaged and froze; some we ran and upset. Being wet made us even colder. It was a bad experience. At that time I didn't know the names of any of the rapids; later when they became familiar to me: Satan's Gut, Dirty Devil, Dark Canyon, I decided they were extremely well-named.

After a day and a half of this we finally rounded a bend and there was Hite. I have to admit I was never so glad to see anything in my life. From Hite, a narrow dirt road wound its way to the highway. Hite itself was a desolate place in those days, the only inhabited spot in hundreds of square miles of desert. At that time I doubt if more than a hundred people came to Hite in an entire year and not more than three or four people lived there for even a few months.

When we pulled the raft out of the river we found one middle-aged couple at Hite who had come there to spend the winter on the desert. They came down to the river bank to watch us take the raft out of the water. They readily agreed to drive us out to the highway the following day where we could catch a ride back to Richfield, Utah. When I caught a glimpse of their ancient car sitting out behind one of the buildings, I had my doubts that we would make it, but it was either that or walk. Next morning the four of us piled into the car and bumped slowly out over the dirt road. It was rough and steep in spots and sometimes I wondered if the car would make it up the grades. Nineteen miles from Hite the car stalled. The man stepped on the starter—nothing. He stepped on it again—still nothing. Finally he got out and lifted the hood. In a minute he came back and grunted, "Battery's dead."

"We have one at Hite," the woman said.

I just stared at Harry. My aching body completely rejected the idea. We were absolutely exhausted. All we wanted was to head for home. Believe me, it was a temptation to leave them there in the desert and hike on out to the highway ourselves.

Deep down, however, I knew I couldn't do it and neither could Harry. With a sigh we nodded, climbed out of the car and started trudging back toward the river. It was almost noon the next day before we struggled back to the car with the battery. Once the man installed it, the car started without difficulty and the couple dropped us off at the highway several hours later.

Once there, we caught a ride to Richfield, raft and all, and from there I took the bus back to Los Angeles.

After that Harry and I parted company as far as river running was concerned. We hiked together some after that and explored Glen Canyon but we never ran the Grand Canyon together.

The following summer I began running the rapids of the Grand Canyon by myself in my own ten-man raft. I couldn't, of course, run the rapids themselves without upsetting. I could either portage around the rapids, or line through (lower the raft through on a rope). Both are hard work and I found I hated it. I didn't enjoy deflating the raft, struggling with it up over the rocks, then pumping it up again. And I found it physically exhausting to lower that raft through a raging rapid.

Then I began to run a few rapids in my raft and portage others. The problem was that I never seemed to select the right ones to run. Finally I decided to just run them all and if I upset, then that's the way it was.

I spent the next three years doing this. I had a lot to learn about the river and I enjoyed seeing it in every mood. I was also anxious to see the rapids under every water condition, to learn where the rocks were and to discover how the water reacted at various levels. During those years I ran the Grand Canyon from Lee's Ferry to Lake Mead at least twenty times, and began to really understand the ways of the water. After I decided to start running the Grand Canyon in my own raft I thought that it would be easy to find people to run the river with me. After all, I had been hiking, for a number of years, with an active group

Running Lava Falls—before, during, after. One of the most ferocious pits on the Colorado, "The Hole," as we call it, is so mean that each operator seems to have a different horror story to tell about it.

of people who seemed to love outdoor sports. River rafting didn't seem to me to be too far removed from rock climbing, cross-country skiing or even hiking. The only one of that group that I could convince to go with me, however, was Elgin Pierce, a friend who had hiked and rock climbed with me several years before.

I will never forget that first trip in the ten-man raft. We left Lee's Ferry, July 1, 1951, and headed down canyon. I managed to run Badger Creek Rapid, Houserock Rapid and several others without trouble. They were, of course, exciting in a small

boat, but I hit the tongue just right and we swept through without overturning on a back wave. The second day was a repeat of the first. At this point, Elgin began to relax. He had imagined all sorts of horrors which just hadn't materialized.

On that third morning we ran a couple of small rapids without trouble, then we swung around a bend and began to approach Hance, one of the worst rapids on the river. Hance, on this trip, was a horrible, roaring nightmare. The water, frothing and white, rolled in full boil with huge waves crashing sideways into the big rocks.

The holes that day were the wickedest I think I've ever seen. Most were at least twenty feet deep, easily deep enough to completely swallow a ten-man raft.

We started through calmly enough. I swung right since the tongue at Hance comes in from that direction. The waves began to rock us, gently at first, then harder and harder. We missed the first hole and I relaxed. Suddenly a huge hole loomed directly in front of us. I couldn't possibly avoid it . . . woosh . . . the front end of the raft dipped, a giant wave loomed above us, and all at once the raft tilted sickeningly and hung there suspended.

"Hang on," I shouted.

Suddenly Elgin panicked, struggled to stand up, then threw himself violently from the boat. Time stood still. The raft bounced twice then began to settle quietly into the waves. I grabbed for the oars to bring myself into shore and felt sick. Elgin, I realized, had taken one oar with him on his way out. I was now helpless on the river. By that time the current had grabbed Elgin and had taken him swiftly into the backwater. Out of the corner of my eye I could see him climbing out on shore.

I was trapped now. A swift back current caught the raft, taking me forcefully toward a rock wall. I couldn't avoid it. Suddenly the raft swept underneath the rock, hung, then flipped upside down. I was in the water now with a fierce current propelling me around and around in a circle. How would I get to shore? I had no idea. Soon I discovered that by pulling on the rope running around the raft I could make it move in any direction. On the first few tries I scooted farther from shore. Finally I began to edge the raft closer and

closer to the bank. I was now nearing a large rock. I waited, lunged, caught the rock and hung on. What a predicament!

Here I was holding the raft, with my feet, next to the rock, while the current tried to pull the raft back into the river. My legs began to ache. I couldn't hang on much longer. I either had to give up the boat and climb out on the rock or let go of the rock and take my chances with the raft.

Just when I was ready to jump back on the raft I heard a yell. I looked around to see Elgin waving to me from the highest point.

"Come on," I beckoned frantically.

When he started toward the river my heart sank. He was headed toward the water above me. The fierce current in this backwater ran in the opposite direction from the current of the river. If you entered upriver you would be swept outward toward the main current. I was positive that Elgin was now on his way downriver. But somehow a miracle occurred. Elgin swept outward about seventy feet, then shot downriver. Instead of continuing on in the main current the backwater caught him and brought him back almost beside me. As he grabbed the raft with one hand I could only stare at him in amazement. Now he worked himself around until he could grab the bow line and toss it to me. Together we tied the boat to the rock and I let go with my feet.

Our troubles, however, were far from over. The boat was upside down. A line ran through all the neoprene food bags holding them against the floor of the raft. To remove one food bag you had to untie the entire line.

"Don't try to get them," I told Elgin. "We'll just have to go hungry. It will be dark soon, just climb up here."

I reached down then and helped him up on my narrow perch. That rock was no bigger than a small table which meant we would have to sit up all night. Suddenly I heard a thump. I looked down beside the rock and there was our missing oar—almost a repeat of the Powell expedition experience on Hance. Their lost oar had come back to them in the current. That night I couldn't help thinking that fate has a funny way of making things happen.

Next morning we turned the raft over, untied the bags, ate breakfast, then started on downriver. Not far downstream we rounded a bend and came smack on Sockdolager, another large rapid. I can remember that scene to this day. Elgin hung on to the raft for dear life with his eyes popping out and screamed, "Oh, my God, a waterfall!"

"For gosh sake," I shouted back, "hang on this time." The raft tipped slightly, then shot through without trouble and a short time later we arrived at Phantom Ranch about ninety miles from Lee's Ferry.

Phantom Ranch was a resort on the bottom of the Grand Canyon where people could ride down on muleback or hike from the canyon rim and spend the night. There were overnight accommodations there, a swimming pool and a place to buy ice cream, beer, and some supplies.

At one time I used to stop at Phantom Ranch on a regular basis and people would come down from the rim to join my trips. Now, however, the Park Service is apparently trying to limit the use of the resort, so river runners are no longer allowed to stop except in an emergency. I thought maybe Elgin would leave me here and hike out to the South Rim of the Grand Canyon, but he didn't. He thought about it awhile, then decided to continue on downriver.

Below this, the river contained some 180 miles of rapids, some much rougher than the ones we had come through. Trying to run them in that single ten-man raft, we upset a number of times. Elgin never did learn to hang on and he took a freelance swim on practically every rapid. Staying with the raft always seemed natural for me, but for some reason there are people like Elgin who just can't seem to learn. After we got back to Las Vegas, I asked him if he'd like to go again that following summer. "You're crazy," he told me. "I'll never go on that river again." He did, but not until years later.

From 1947 to mid-season 1954 I ran from two to six trips a season. Sometimes I would take a few passengers, but most of the time I went down the river by myself. Toward the end of those years, when six to eight people would show up to go with me, I thought I had a real crowd. Among those, with the exception of my brother Paul and one young girl, no one ever went a second time. I'm not sure why I stayed with the river. All I can say is that from the moment I discovered this way of life I loved it and wanted to share it with the whole world. To this day I wouldn't dream of doing anything else.

During those pioneering years my brother Paul joined me intermittently. He had by now grown to a huge six feet five inches and could charm almost anyone he came in contact with. Paul didn't really share my interest in the river but he did have an active interest in geology and mining so the idea of prospecting the canyon fascinated him.

"You never stay with anything very long, Georgie," he told me, "so if I intend to explore the canyon I'd better go before you move on to something else."

It was true that I was restless and had never stayed with any one thing very long up to this point. But I knew that this river life was what I had always been searching for, and that I would be running rivers until I died. I couldn't convince Paul of this, however, so I just encouraged him to go with me when he could. I took him a couple of times the second year I ran the Grand Canyon and he learned to row a ten-man raft. He became so skillful in fact, that sometimes he would row a second boat, in addition to mine, carrying a few passengers. At other times he just went along to prospect. He loved to collect stories about lost mines, lost gold strikes and he was never happier than when he was trying to check out one of them.

One time near the junction of Tapeats Creek and Thunder River, Paul and a partner stopped to look into a story about two prospectors who had discovered an immense deposit of placer gold in a sand bar.

The rumor was that the miners took out several hundred thousand dollars in gold when the Colorado River rose during flood stage and covered the sandbar. When the water receded a few weeks later, both the sandbar and the remaining gold had completely disappeared. Paul wanted to see if he could discover the source of the gold and see if the story was true. He did find

traces of gold but he couldn't find the outcropping he was looking for.

Later Paul staked an asbestos claim near there in what was then National Forest. It turned out to be of exceptional quality and worth at least seventeen hundred dollars a ton, but Paul never attempted to mine it. Frequently I would drop him off somewhere in mid-canyon. He would hike and prospect for a couple of weeks, then, when I came through on the next trip, I would pick him up.

I went down the river so many times during those years that the trips began to blend together in my memory. One, however, stands out vividly.

On this trip, four people had joined me at Lee's Ferry to run the rapids and share expenses. Generally, I didn't take teenagers in those days but I had been talked into taking a lanky seventeen-year-old boy whom I'll call Bill. Most teenagers really enjoy the river and Bill was no exception. He was so scatterbrained, though, and had so much energy that I never knew what to expect next. As usual I talked about safety and told everyone what to do if we upset.

"Don't let go of the raft. If you find yourself under the boat, don't worry; there is an air pocket there. Stay put until you hear me yell; then take a big breath and work yourself out hand-over-hand."

Everybody nodded that they understood. But when I began the trip at Lee's Ferry I was quite apprehensive. Everything went well the first couple of hours and I began to relax.

Then we reached Cave Springs Rapid, a mild rapid a little over twenty-five miles from Lee's Ferry. We started through easily enough, when out of nowhere, a giant wave hit the raft. It flew up and up, then hung in the balance for a minute; then it turned upside down. Irene, my woman passenger, remembered her lessons well and hung onto the boat. But Bill, in a moment of panic, forgot everything I had said. Suddenly there he was yelling for help at the top of his lungs and swimming wildly upstream. My brother, coming just behind, quickly pulled Bill into his boat.

At this point I guess I should have known that this incident was an omen of things to come. Next morning we started down the river in bright sunshine, but within a few hours large fluffy clouds began to build over the canyon. By one o'clock, dark, threatening clouds covered most of the sky. I didn't pay much attention, since we frequently have storms along the Grand Canyon during the summer months. When I began to hear loud, rolling thunder I wasn't too surprised. Then it began to rain lightly. A half hour later the rain was coming down in solid sheets, lightning split the sky, and a mist began to rise from the water. We were now about five miles above Grapevine Rapid. The day had turned dark gray, the mist had turned to fog and was getting thicker by the minute.

By the time we reached Grapevine I could hardly see the cliffs on either side of the river. Hail began to pound the rafts and hundreds of rocks began to pour off the cliffs into the river. We really couldn't see the rapid, but somehow we bumped through it as the fog closed in completely. I had intended to land at Phantom Ranch, but in the fog I went right past. Miles below Phantom Ranch I finally managed to pull into the bank and land. I wasn't quite

In those early days we set another record with the big boats everytime we took a new party downriver.

47

sure where we were then and to this day I haven't been able to find the spot again.

All of us spread out under a narrow rock overhang and tried to find someplace to sleep. I didn't spend a very restful night because I picked a rock ledge where I had to curl up like a doughnut.

The next morning Bill came out from somewhere in back carrying a miner's bedroll and a carved oar. "There's some dynamite back there too," he said, "but I can't move it." Paul took charge at this point and discovered Bill had been picking around the edges of some crystallized dynamite. Paul immediately ripped off the hardhat he was wearing, filled it with water and soaked the dynamite. After that he eased it out and threw it in the river. That, I figured, was a pretty close call. Paul became quite sick from breathing the nitrous oxide fumes from the dynamite and had to lay over an extra day. I never did learn any more about the miner who abandoned that equipment. Had he left the river or simply died up there in one of the side canyons? This is typical of some of the mysteries I've run into on the Grand Canyon. The river has many secrets, most of which it will never reveal.

I have to admit that despite the problems, Bill added a great deal to that trip. He had a tremendous imagination and was always making up wild stories. I often wonder if he became a writer.

A few nights after this incident we were camped on a sandbar some miles downstream. Irene had placed her sleeping bag fairly near the water and sometime during the night I heard a yell from her direction.

I came running with my flashlight. "What's wrong?" I asked.

Irene looked sheepish, "The river came up, and I was in such a hurry to get away that I let the water carry away my air mattress."

Next morning, back on the water, Bill stared off into space for a long time. Finally he said, "Georgie, what would you do if Irene had slept too long, and when you ran down to the river both Irene and her bedroll had disappeared, and—" At this point I turned away shaking my head. But I remember his words to this day: "What if Irene had been swept down the river?"

During those pioneer years I guess I explored nearly all of the side canyons and the escape routes. I also used to stop at Nankoweap Creek ruins regularly. This is a scrambling half-mile climb up the talus from the river to some well-preserved Indian ruins at the foot of a sheer wall. You can see about four sites here; there are about two hundred sites in the canyon. In my years of hiking the canyon I have discovered many of them. Judging by the number of ruins I have seen, the canyon at one time must have been teeming with Indians.

Another of my favorite sites along the river is the Copper Blossom Mine near Mile Sixty-Five. Paul and I used to stop here, climb to the mine and explore the shafts. Usually we would take a lunch and spend hours following the maze underground. They are full of water now, but I have many pleasant memories of our early days there.

At Copper Blossom Mine I discovered a well-preserved bellows and wooden

Dan Davis was the first park ranger to go down the river with me, and it was a great pleasure to have him on the trip.

saddle. I always made sure that no one touched them because I felt they were a part of the legend of the canyon and should remain there. The rangers, however, removed these a number of years ago after I pointed them out. I would have much preferred that they leave them alone.

From 1945 to 1954 practically no one else was running the river. Frequently I made entire trips without seeing another soul. During that time, besides myself, there was only one other person running the canyon consistently. That was Norman

Nevills, a tall lean man who ran the river in a modified wooden boat called a catarac boat. He was running the river commercially and charged about a thousand dollars a trip. I have to admit that seemed like a lot of money and that I often envied him for it.

Norman was extremely fussy on the river. He and his boatmen would walk to where they could overlook a rapid; then they would hold a conference. They would nod and point for at least a half hour. You would have thought that they were working out a tremendous problem. Sometimes I think he purposely made rapid running harder than it really was.

Norman would never quite believe that a woman could tackle the Colorado River. I understand that he was quite upset when I started running rafts through the rapids while he was still lining or portaging his boats through most of them. Norman and I weren't really too friendly. We talked now and then, but generally he would just nod when he saw me and go on with whatever he was doing.

Although Norman Nelvills paid attention to detail on the river, he wasn't quite so meticulous when it came to flying. I've seen him fly into places I certainly would never try to take a plane. Norman lived at Mexican Hat on the San Juan River and took off and landed on an air strip that extended to the canyon edge. One day while attempting to take off, he couldn't seem to pull up and crashed into the far canyon wall and died. After watching him fly I can't say that I was really too surprised.

There were a few other adventurers

In the early years we launched at Mexican Hat, Utah, to start the San Juan River trip. This was where Norman Nevills crashed his plane on take-off.

who ran the river during those early years: "Dock" Martson and Ed Hudson, Jim and Bob Riggs, Jimmy Jordan and Rod Sanderson.

Then, there was Bert Loper. He had been running wooden boats for a long time on the Glen Canyon and occasionally I ran into him on the river. In 1949 he died while running Twenty-Four-and-a-Half-Mile Rapid in the Grand Canyon. Bert Loper loved the Colorado River, but he had been in very poor health for several years before his death. The boat he rowed on that last trip was designed for Glen Canyon and Bert well knew that it wouldn't stand up in the rapids of the Grand Canyon. In addition he wouldn't let anyone else ride in the same boat with him on that last trip. His death was listed officially as a heart attack, but I personally have some unanswered questions about it.

When I came through the canyon on my first trip after his death I came on his boat several miles downstream from Twenty-Four-and-a-Half-Mile Rapid and pulled it farther up on the bank so the next high water wouldn't sweep it on down the river.

Those years from 1945 to 1954 were very satisfying ones. I finally discovered something I really wanted to do, and every time I ran the Colorado River I simply wanted to turn right around and run it again. The one thing I felt I needed to do from here on, was to find a way to take more people with me on the river. Up to this time I just never had more than a handful who wanted to share the experience. As I finished my first ten years on the river, this problem—and at that point it had begun to assume the proportions of a problem in my mind—began to nag at me more and more.

Opening the White Water Experience to Everyone

*I*f there is any one thing that I learned during those early pioneering years, it was that I wasn't going to get very many people to go with me on the river as long as I kept flipping my fellow adventurers out in the water on most rapids. The average person just wasn't going to take that kind of abuse.

I'm not sure, even now, that I really understood how they felt. Those early years in Chicago had been so severe and my mother's formula for coping with life so deeply ingrained that I just accepted conditions as they were. Actually I didn't mind upsetting. After all I had swum part of the Colorado River twice in a life jacket and had run the Grand Canyon at least one hundred times, more times than anyone else in the world. I also had swum each and every rapid at least once. Having a raft flip in a rapid was just a way of life for me, and an enjoyable one at that. Most people I talked to at that time, however, wouldn't agree. They said, "It's too dangerous, Georgie. You've got to be crazy to run the river that way."

That was an opinion shared not only by my fellow potential adventurers, but practically everyone else. Frequently even experienced river people would look at me and shake their heads. "That crazy woman is at it again."

I really didn't care what they thought. But it did bother me that I couldn't get anyone to join me. Most trips I averaged four to five people. When I got eight, I thought I had a crowd. If as many as sixteen had decided to go on any of my early trips I would have been the most surprised person on the river.

I had by this time decided that I wanted to make rafting on the Colorado River a commercial venture. I still had to work winters in Los Angeles to finance the summers on the river. During the first ten years I mostly took people on a share-the-expense basis. But from the early 1950s on I hoped to spend more time exploring other rivers, and I knew that to finance these explorations I'd have to make the Colorado trips as commercial as possible. My feelings, however, went far deeper than this. I ran rivers and rapids because they excited me. Actually it is hard for me to describe what the river and the canyon really mean to me. I'm not a church-going person but you might say I felt the experience I had running rapids was almost religious.

People will tell you that the wilderness has emotions; indeed it does. The Grand Canyon alone is a moving experience. The depth and distance and scale of the canyon is almost beyond imagination—the average person just wouldn't believe it. There are cliffs and buttes and towers and arches with colors that run from white to black to brilliant red and everything else in between. Once you enter the world of that canyon on the Colorado River you are alone; I mean completely alone. There

were many times during those first years that I would run the entire 280 miles from Lee's Ferry to Lake Mead without seeing another soul. Imagine, if you can, the state of being completely cut off and unable to speak to another person for from two to three weeks at a time.

The rapids, of course, are their own experience. There is something super exhilarating about pitting yourself against the force of that moving water. Maybe I can express it this way: I have over the years developed a kidding relationship with the men who are my boatmen on the river. Frequently they will make a joke in front of others about taking me off somewhere and giving me a sexual thrill. I always tell them that anytime they can equal the experience of running Lava or Crystal Rapids—I'm ready. Truthfully, there is nothing in life quite as exciting as shooting a wild, surging rapid. And I know very few people who can run the rapids of any wild river and not come back changed.

The more I began to understand this and to feel the pressures of city life the more I felt compelled to share this experience with others. I wasn't thinking, however, of sharing the experience with three or four other people but hundreds and even thousands.

For some reason in those early years, I believed that since the river required strenuous activity, people who worked with their hands—plumbers, carpenters, construction workers and others like them —were the ones who would enjoy a river trip. Consequently, I spent most of my time talking river to this type of person. It wasn't until years later that I realized that when these people go on vacation they want to dress up, but that doctors, lawyers, nurses, teachers and other professionals enjoyed the challenge of the outdoors. I find that most of the people who go on the river with me today belong to these groups.

To add to my problems, very few people were interested in exploring the Colorado or any other river. All activities seem to run in fads. And none of the outdoor sports such as hiking, mountain climbing or river running were very popular in those days. In the face of this disinterest I could have given up. For some reason, however, I didn't. It seemed that the desire to share the river experience with others became stronger with each and every trip. By the early 1950s it had become almost an obsession. I had to find a way to make running the Colorado River easier and more popular.

My mind went crazy in those years and I dreamed up some of the wildest schemes you ever heard of. I discarded most of them, but I did manage to try out a few on the river. The first idea I put into operation proved to be a real Rube Goldberg, workable, but absolutely impractical. I kept thinking of the way a raft turns upside down in a rapid and flips everyone in it out in the water. But if I had put another raft on top of the first, when it turned over everyone would simply drop into the second raft and float on through the rapid.

During the middle of one of my trips I dropped this bombshell on my brother. His reaction was instant. "You're out of your mind. Even if it does work you haven't got anything."

"We'll try it anyway," I said.

We placed my boat upside down on top of his and lashed the bow of my raft to the rear of his. No matter which way the river tossed us, then we still had an upright boat.

We then pushed the two rafts free of the river bank and prepared to climb in. Paul forced the tubes apart and squeezed his big body into the small opening between the two rafts. I followed, making space for myself where I could. Actually we needed extra room to try this experiment, so I had pushed the baggage farther back. I knew that the minute the boat flipped, water taken in while running the rapid would pour from the top raft to the lower one. If we remained face down our noses would be six to eight inches under water. It was therefore essential to squirm around and turn over. With the raft pulled up on the beach this was a difficult enough task. But in a raft bouncing up and down with two thrashing people getting tangled in each other's arms and legs it became almost impossible. Paul was so much bigger than I was that he really had me squeezed into a corner.

We were on our way now, bouncing through those waves like a dancing cork. What a strange sensation that was! The cramped quarters and semi-darkness seemed to exaggerate every motion. At every dip the waves exploded through the small opening between the two rafts soaking us to the skin. Suddenly, without warning, we slammed headlong into a giant wave. The rafts shuddered, stood on end, started to settle, stood on end again and flipped upside down. Water poured through the opening. As the rafts exchanged positions all the water in the bottom raft came crashing down on us. I squirmed wildly to turn upright with Paul twisting to get his own head out of water, but I found movement almost impossible. Finally I sat up and tried to catch my breath. Paul was lying across me breathing hard. The raft was floating free below the rapid. We had made it. Lying there in the semi-darkness in eight inches of water I felt tremendous.

"So what?" Paul snapped. "Georgie, no one else will go down the river in that contraption. I only went because you talked me into it. You might as well forget the whole thing right now." Paul was right. Very few people would let themselves be sandwiched in between two rafts and flipped upside down in a rapid.

I quit experimenting for quite awhile after that and just concentrated on running the river. It was the same old thing. Almost nobody wanted to share the experience.

Every time I flipped on a rapid after that, or portaged, I would try to figure out how to eliminate both flipping and portaging. Both of these alternatives were rapidly becoming unacceptable.

At this point I was in my tenth season on the Colorado River. I knew I was long overdue for a change, but I didn't know that this change, when it came, would completely revolutionize rafting on the Colorado River.

I had for the past several months been working on the idea of tying three ten-man rafts together. I believed that if I tied these rafts side-by-side they would go through much rougher water without upsetting and in the high water the three boats would balance each other. I reasoned that the boats not affected by wave action would act as ballast.

On the trip for which I made these changes, we left Lee's Ferry about two in the afternoon of July 6, running three separate rafts, each with its own boatman. We ran that day without much difficulty. A ten-man raft would flip now and then on a rapid, but I expected that. We portaged Hance, Sockdolager and Grapevine, taking almost half a day on each. My dissatisfaction grew at each delay. I was rapidly coming to the point where I was ready to try my new idea. About noon on the fourth day, as I stood looking down at one of the rapids, I made a decision. I was going to tie those ten-man rafts together today and run that rapid. I had mentioned this to my boatmen several times before, but they had decided that I really wasn't serious.

"Bring the boats over here," I told them. "I'm going to lash them together." I could see the questioning look on their faces. *That crazy woman is at it again.*

I took some rope and simply tied the boats together by the handles. I had some serious doubts about this tie, but I had to start somewhere. That final craft looked absolutely ugly and unmanageable, but I was determined, so we pushed it in the water and shoved off. As we swept down the tongue of that rapid I had second thoughts; maybe I'd hang on the rocks and tear the raft to pieces.

I didn't try to head the bow downstream as I would a single raft, but with one oarsman on each side we swung that whole awkward boat at right angles to the current. It was working. We surged through two huge waves without difficulty, the three rafts stabilizing each other. Then, bam! The front raft slammed into a huge wave and just disappeared. Suddenly the raft I was sitting in simply left the water, propelled by a violent wave and catapulted up, up, up, and over the other two rafts. I hung on for dear life.

All at once, there I was, hanging about four feet off the water looking the boatman on the far side right in the eye. He looked startled and seemed to be saying, "Georgie, what are you doing out there?"

Obviously, I had tied the boats too loosely. The handles just weren't going to work, but I had seen enough to know that I was heading in the right direction. I immediately pulled into shore and began retying. I untied the handles and looped the rope around the seats.

The seats in those surplus ten-man boats were the toughest things I have ever seen. You could tie around them and expect it to hold. That isn't true of the boats today. Those original boats were navy surplus and they were made of exceptionally high-quality material. When these began to disappear from the market, private manufacturers began making rafts designed exclusively for river running. These rafts, however, are just not the same quality as those early ones and today I wouldn't dare tie around the seats on the newer rafts. In those days, however, it worked. Once I had the boats all tied together again I pulled the rope as tight as I could get it. Then we shoved off again.

We shot through Horn Creek Rapid like it wasn't there and went on to run every rapid from there to Lake Mead including Lava Falls. It was a whole new way of running a river. Of course, in the more violent water a raft could still flip back over the others, but it was virtually impossible to turn the entire three-boat combination upside down in a rapid. At first, we rowed the three boats and surprisingly enough, with a boatman rowing on either side, that monstrously awkward boat proved extremely maneuverable.

Now for the first time, I had a method that would let me run all rapids without portaging. I was the first river adventurer in the world to try this method. That may not sound like much of a change, but up until the summer of 1954 no one had been able to run the large rapids consistently without upsetting. Now, after putting the three boats together we could take the largest of rapids in relative safety.

In the beginning many people were apprehensive about the three-boat. In fact I even had trouble convincing my own boatmen that this was the way to run rapids. By 1955 I had gotten most of my boatmen to go along with the idea. But one of them, called Fred, was still apprehensive. He did, however, run the river in the three-boat until he came to Horn Rapid. On this trip the water was fairly low and that rapid looked fierce. Fred took one look and said, "No way will I run those boats through that monster."

"Okay," I said. "Tie them up, and when I run my boat through I'll come back and turn them loose. We'll pick them up somewhere downstream in a backwater."

I took all the people through on my boat, then I came back and released his. That three-boat went through that rapid like it knew just where to go. I had discovered long before that if you start a boat right it will almost pick its own path through a rapid. Seeing that raft go through without his guiding it, seemed to deflate his ego. After all, he had thought he was quite a boatman by then. I must say that I didn't have a bit of trouble with Fred after that.

Once the other river runners began to realize how well this idea worked they also started running the three-boat combination themselves. This combination soon became known as a G-boat, named after me, and soon all sorts of three-boat combinations began appearing on the river. Later Jack Cury also developed a technique of lashing long turned-up tubes together. These were called J-boats, after him, and today all commercial rafts on the Colorado River are a variation of either the G- or the J-boats.

I had also considered for a long time the possibility of using motors on the river. Once I started running the G-boats, motors became even more useful. While the three boats were surprisingly maneuverable with oars, they were more so with a small motor. So during the winter of 1954 I bought several 10 hp motors for use the following summer. Besides contributing to the maneuverability of the rafts, the motors also speeded the trip up by several days.

The simple act of linking those three rafts together was a real breakthrough, but I still wasn't satisfied. I could now run all rapids easily, but even at that, only the most adventurous still wanted to go. I wanted to take families and children and older people. Why, I asked myself, should anyone be deprived of what I considered to

After I came up with the cockeyed notion of lashing the three boats together I found I could run almost any rapid without upsetting.

be the ultimate experience? I brooded over that all the next winter. Up to that point most people on the river had some idea that I was crazy. But the solution to this problem that I dreamed up really convinced them that this was a fact.

Several years before, I had seen newsreel shots of the Army Corps of Engineers erecting pontoon bridges with elongated rafts like oval pontoons. I discovered several of these in a Los Angeles surplus yard, and the more I looked at them, the more I felt they might just be the answer. I could lash three together to make one huge raft. I also decided that in the oval interior of each of these rafts I would place a long inflated tube that I called a sausage. This would give me tremendous flotation. It would take large waves and big water

Different moments on a river trip: hitting rough water; playing around with the air mattresses in clear water; getting really, really wet.

without difficulty and give me the safest boat on the river.

That's what I believed. Now I had to try it out. I bought the pontoons and the sausages, loaded them into a large stake-bed truck and headed for Lee's Ferry. Once on the river I lashed everything together just as I had done with the three-boats. Getting the right tie was a trial-and-error process. I tied the rafts several ways before I found a lashing that worked best. For

that first trip, I also lashed a 10 hp motor on the back of the middle raft and carried two more motors as back-up.

When I got the whole thing tied together I rounded up some people and we pushed it into the water. The old timers just gawked. I had to admit that the bridge pontoon raft was a real eyepopper. It was thirty-seven feet long and about twenty-seven feet wide, the biggest, most awkward raft ever seen on the Colorado River.

"You're not going to get me on that," my brother told me. "Georgie, you're going too far. That monster will pile on the rocks at every rapid. You'll never control it."

"Never mind," I said. "People will think it's safe and right now that's what counts."

I spent the first few miles getting used to running what I was already calling the "big boat." After running the little rafts for so long it felt like a battleship and even though it looked awkward, it didn't handle that way. With the small motor lashed to the back of the middle raft it maneuvered unusually well. When I came to Badger Creek, the first rapid on the river after Lee's Ferry, I just headed down the tongue and took it straight on. The big boat rolled right through that rapid almost like it wasn't there; those three lashed pontoons were handling beautifully and the passengers hardly got wet at all.

After I shot a few of the bigger rapids those first few days and made it look easy, my brother Paul decided that maybe I wasn't so crazy after all. He had taken quite a pounding that trip and had flipped on almost every rapid, so he decided to put his ten-man raft up front on top of the big boat. With his raft there I could hardly see the water so he stood up front and hollered directions, "Go right Georgie! Go left!"

That didn't work very well. I would misunderstand and hit the rocks, or I wouldn't hear what Paul said and turn into a wall, but somehow we got through.

With the boats tied together I still had several problems. Those big boats took in an awful lot of water in a rapid and it took forever to bail one of those huge pontoons. I was also having trouble with the small motor. Lashed to the outside, it didn't seem to give me good control over the raft. Every time I had to turn the raft, someone had to grab me by the ankles so I could lean out over those huge tubes to reach the motor handle. The driftwood on the river also made using the motor a big problem. In those days before Glen Canyon Dam, huge amounts of driftwood would pour out of the canyons and create a tremendous barrier. It could, for instance, trap a raft in the backwater and make it difficult to pull the raft out into the main current. Sometimes the logs would come in and crush a motor or the motor would hit a large piece of driftwood and break a sheer pin. I had taken three motors with me that trip but within a short time all three were badly damaged.

The idea of the "big boat," however, was a sound one. All I had to do was work out the major bugs. That winter I thought a lot about the problem. Finally I decided that I had to cut the neoprene bottom out of the center pontoon. If I then moved the motor inside, the tube would protect the motor from the driftwood.

I agonized over that decision for months. I couldn't stand to destroy all that good rubber. Finally I took a big knife and just started hacking away until I had cut the bottom out of the middle oval. Then I asked Elgin Pierce, who had run the river with me on my first raft trip down the Grand Canyon and who was also a custom cabinet maker, to take a look at the raft. "Build me a motor mount and a platform to stand on," I told him. "It's got to be able to take a lot of buffeting."

Elgin knew exactly what to do since he had seen the river at its worst. The motor mount he designed and built lasted for years. Those motor mounts of Elgin's were constructed so well that when I had to replace several of them recently I said to the carpenters, "Don't question why he did something a certain way. Just do it like he did."

That solved my motor problem but I still had some difficulties running the rapids. I had cut the bottom out of the middle boat but I hadn't cut the bottoms out of those two outside pontoons. Now every time I ran a rapid one of them filled with water and forced me to run sideways. Finally I cut the bottoms out of these pontoons and raised the sausages to provide a back rest for the passengers. This gave me the most luxurious craft on the river.

The problem now was to let people know I had this big, safe raft. That winter I blew the pontoons up in my garage, tied them together to make the big boat, and invited some people from a river movie showing to come home with me and look at the rafts. It worked, and seventeen people signed up for my next river trip. After that, more and more people began to come on the river. I now had a raft that really looked safe to people and also had so much flotation that it could take anything the river could possibly throw at it and come through without any difficulty at all. Several incidents on the river since that time have convinced me that I was right in sticking with it until I had developed a boat with that amount of flotation.

In 1955, the very first year that I ran the river in the big boat, I decided to put it to the ultimate test and run it right through the huge hole on Lava Falls. I will never forget that day. I came up on the rapid without even slowing down, caught the tongue and headed straight for the hole. It was a frothing monster and for a minute I wondered if I had made a mistake. The raft rose slightly then suddenly dove straight down into that hole. I shut off the motor and was engulfed instantly by a twenty-foot wall of water. Time stood still. Then we burst through the other side of the wave and ran the rest of the way without difficulty. The big boat had come through with flying colors. If I had tried to run anything smaller through the hole that day I'm sure I would have been in trouble. That was the first incident. The second one occurred twelve years later farther up river. During the winter of 1967 a huge storm swept through the Grand Canyon. Crystal Creek, about one hundred miles downriver from Lee's Ferry, really turned loose and swept huge boulders out of the side canyons and into the river. Overnight it turned Crystal from a miscellaneous minor ripple into one of the most treacherous and most dangerous rapids on the river. The river in high water just barely covers the biggest boulders. In low water, the boulders themselves sit exposed in the raging current. When I left on that first Grand Canyon trip in April I knew that a major storm had swept the canyon but I didn't know it had done any damage.

I pulled into Phantom Ranch the afternoon of the third day. The next morning I pushed on downriver with twenty people on board. I ran several rapids easily, then I rounded the bend just above Crystal Rapid and caught my breath. I was now looking at one of the most dangerous stretches of rapids I think I've ever seen.

"Hang on," I shouted. I instinctively headed to the right. We teetered for a moment then went roller-coasting through the rapid just skimming the edge of the rocks. It was close, but I got through.

Today I run Crystal to the left because if the motor fails on the right side we will hang on the rocks. That happened to another boat a few years ago and the passengers had to wait all night for the water to come up and free their raft. The left side sometimes becomes quite shallow, but it provides the best route through the rapid. I can predict a time, though, when I will get stuck trying to run the left side and have to untie the three pontoons on the big boat and run them through separately. In a ten-man raft or even the three-boat, that first trip through Crystal might have turned into a disaster. With the big boat it just became an exciting experience.

The final incident on the river which convinced me of the value of the big boat, occurred just a few years ago in extremely low water. I pulled into Lee's Ferry ready to go down canyon and received a tremendous shock. That water was lower than I had ever seen it before, probably streaming at under 3000 cubic feet a second.

"We'll wait for awhile and see if the water comes up," I told the people with me. "We may take twelve to fifteen days to reach Temple Bar in this low water, however, so I suggest that if anyone has to meet a deadline on the other end, you don't go on the trip."

One doctor left, and everyone else stayed. Later that day it became apparent the river was just not going to rise. "I've got the biggest outfit on the river," I told

Though it looks like the edge of a waterfall, we're actually just about to plunge into a whirlpool, in which the greatest danger is the swirling logs keeping us company.

Here we're making camp for the night and I must admit it doesn't look very soft. Most of the time, though, we are able to find large, flat camps where it's easy to get a good night's sleep.

my boatmen. "Three huge boats and two big sausages. I can cut two of those boats and still run. We have enough food for a twenty-day trip, so let's go."

With that we shoved off. The first seven miles I ran with absolutely no trouble at all; then we came to Badger Creek Rapid. I've never seen anything like it. It looked like a boat convention. There must have been twenty boatmen sitting around trying to decide what to do. A few were throwing little sticks in the water to see where the current took them.

Badger Creek is not a big rapid, as rapids go on the Colorado River, but it is a wide rapid and has a lot of rocks. In low water you can hang up in at least a dozen places.

"I'm not going to stop," I told everyone. "Here we go." I came in on the tongue just right, bounced across some smooth rocks and shot right on through.

When we reached Houserock Rapid, nine miles below Badger Creek, the other boats were piled up waiting. Houserock Rapid can easily fool you. Years ago a storm brought in some large boulders on the right side of Houserock and caused the current to swing to the left. This current then created a large sharp undercut in the rocks on the left side. If you come in too close to that undercut you will upset the smaller boats and cut the big boat. I had seen this rapid in all kinds of water conditions so I knew exactly what to watch for here. I simply kept well away from the undercut and went right on through without a problem.

After I made it through safely, all the rest of the boats came through. Later some of the boatmen caught up with me. "What are you trying to do, Georgie?" they teased me. "Make us look bad?"

I couldn't see any advantage in just sitting above a rapid. I knew the water and I knew the big boat was safe. If I had stuck somewhere I would simply have waited a day or two until the water came up and floated me off the rocks.

Now that I had the three-boat and the big boat I was prepared to tackle any kind of water, anywhere in the world. Later, on other rivers, I was extremely glad I had gone through those developmental years on the Colorado River. I had swum the rapids, tackled them in ten-man rafts, and finally graduated to the larger G-boats. I had tackled all kinds of water conditions ranging from a high of 125,000 cubic feet per second to a low of about 3000. I had seen every rapid at all water levels and knew exactly what to expect from each. All in all, the Colorado River had proved to be an excellent training ground for me.

Conquering Glen Canyon

After I developed the three-boat concept and then the big boat, I began to expand my trips considerably. Now instead of just running the Grand Canyon I would link the trip together with the Upper Colorado and its tributaries. Starting at Green River, Wyoming, I would run the Green through Labyrinth and Stillwater Canyons, through Catarac and Glen and finally through the Grand Canyon to Lake Mead, almost eleven hundred miles.

This extended trip sampled a wide variety of scenery and river conditions and took almost thirty days to complete. The upper portion was pretty much high desert. Labyrinth and Stillwater Canyons contained many colorful plateaus and mesas. In Catarac Canyon the walls became sheer and the river became a wild beast dropping 415 feet in fifty miles to produce a series of what were probably the most exciting rapids in the United States. Glen Canyon was one of the most fantastic areas on the river with tremendous red limestone cliffs, Indian petroglyphs, ruins and unusual formations. There probably isn't an area anywhere in the world like Glen Canyon before they built the dam. Sometimes I would make the entire eleven hundred mile run as one continuous trip. Other times I would break it up going from Green River, Utah to Hite, from Hite to

Marble Canyon, or from Lee's Ferry to Lake Mead.

As a variation of this I would also come down the Escalante or San Juan Rivers to the Colorado River. The Escalante River was fun in high water, but in low water we literally had to push the rafts across the sandbars to the Colorado River. The first trip through, Harry and I hit the flood waters of the Escalante just right and managed to float all the way through without difficulty. The next year, Randall Henderson, publisher of Desert Magazine, and his wife decided to go with me. I had fortunately warned them that we might have to walk some of the way, but I wasn't prepared for what we found. The water ran only a few inches deep, and Harry and I had to push both rafts the entire seventy miles to the Colorado River. I never ran the Escalante River again, but in later years, I often pulled about five miles up the canyon as I came down Glen just to let the people with me see the tapestry-like beauty of the canyon.

The San Juan River was something else. It ran through spectacular red sandstone country with towering spires and some of the most fantastic formations to be seen anywhere. Especially intriguing were the Goosenecks of the San Juan where the river has cut a series of unusual loops that wind snake-like through the desert. People often came on this trip with me just to experience the rugged, almost inaccessible back country, as well as the river itself.

I would pick up my passengers in Marble Canyon, Arizona, pile in the car and a pickup truck and head off on a narrow dirt road across the incredibly beautiful Monument Valley. I always went first in the pickup because I knew that when I came to a difficult spot, the first vehicle would probably get through, but the second would usually become stuck in the sand. When this happened, everybody would pile out. I would unload the shovels and the boards that I always carried and begin to dig the sand out from around the stuck wheel. Finally when I had it clear, I would shove the boards underneath and together we'd push and drive the car out of the sand. This became a vital part of the trip and somehow people were always disappointed when it didn't happen.

The San Juan was an unusual river. During the low water period, many sandbars would appear, making boating difficult. In low water too, the river would break into a number of channels, and finding the right channel could be a problem. I learned early how to deal with this. I would simply run the motor slowly and wait. Invariably someone would say, "What are you doing, Georgie?"

"I'm letting the motor pick the channel."

They wouldn't believe me, but I found that when I ran the motor slowly enough, the boat would automatically find the channel with the most current. After learning this method on the San Juan River, I later used it quite successfully on Lake Mead to pick my way through the driftwood.

In the very early days Harry and I hiked a great deal in Glen Canyon. Glen, at that time, was probably the hottest spot on the river. The sun on that red sandstone turned the side canyons into radiating ovens.

That didn't bother us much, however; I can take heat well and after hiking the canyons as long as we had, we didn't really seem to feel it. By this time, I needed little food and water. I used to take along just a few small cans of tomatoes to eat and found this quite satisfactory. I hiked better and was more alert. I also found that water bothered my stomach while hiking so I seldom drank anything in the canyon.

In Glen, the canyon walls were extremely steep. To protect themselves from enemies, the ancient ones, or Anasazi, as the present day Indians call them, always built their mud buildings under an overhang high up on the canyon walls. To reach them, they had made tiny foot and hand holds called Moki steps which went hundreds of feet straight up the walls. When I saw these I just shook my head. They were so tiny. Did these Indians have smaller feet than the white man? Did they have an unusual sense of balance? Had they perfected some method of climbing I hadn't heard about? I really couldn't figure it out.

By using extreme caution I could climb into most places over these steps. My problem was, however, that I wanted to take people into the side canyons since I felt it would add considerable interest to the river trip. But the Moki steps as they existed were too small. Very few people were even going to try them.

"We're going to have to enlarge those steps," I told Harry. "They'll just never work that way."

He protested at first, then finally agreed I was right. We took a hammer and began to enlarge the backs and edges of several steps. That didn't work. The sand-stone was so brittle that often we'd destroy a whole step. I soon realized that I'd have to go about it the Indian way. So we then took hard smooth rocks and rubbed them back and forth on those steps for hours on end, until we had them just right. In those days I spent so many hours enlarging Moki steps that I often found myself making steps in my dreams.

Actually, it took awhile to get the knack of it. The Moki step itself has a peculiar back slant. I realized that the Indians made them this way to give a better foothold. So we rubbed until we got the backslant just like the Indian steps only several times larger, of course. When we got through they were big enough to provide good foot and hand holds all the way up the cliff.

One of the first places Harry and I opened was Moki Canyon. The canyon itself contained a tremendous collection of ruins. The buildings reminded me of pictures of mud and adobe houses in early Jerusalem built with flat roofs. They literally stair-stepped up the slope in very tight clusters. With little effort I could recognize granaries and a few other buildings. Even after a couple of thousand years some buildings remained in remarkable shape. Others consisted of just a broken wall or two.

I knew that people would really enjoy that canyon. When we finished enlarging the steps, the first groups I took in consisted of Boy Scouts and their leaders. Although I couldn't get a lot of people to go with me in those days, I frequently got a number of Scout troops from the Los Angeles area who wanted to explore the Glen Canyon area.

Since I was a woman, the mothers seemed to feel safer letting their sons go out in the wilderness of Glen Canyon with me. Later I often thought that if only those mothers could have seen their children climbing those high canyon walls they would have quickly changed their minds. I found that the scouts absolutely loved Moki Canyon. If I had let them alone they probably could have spent several days exploring that one canyon alone.

Heights didn't bother me, and I thought nothing of climbing hundreds of feet unprotected up those small Moki steps. Neither did the Scouts. They seemed to have no fear at all. So I guess it was natural that after a couple of years I began to treat these climbs in a matter-of-fact manner. A few years later, however, when I first took the Sierra Club groups into Moki Canyon and started up into those ruins, they let me know in no uncertain terms how unsafe they felt that climb was.

They had been used to utilizing ropes on climbs like this. But because of the great heights of those walls, they couldn't belay their ropes in Moki Canyon.

"You're going to get someone killed up there, Georgie," they told me. "Some day one of your people is just going to peel off that cliff."

I felt at that time they were just being too cautious. Later, however, when I started taking a different type of person into the canyons their message came home rather dramatically.

One spring day in 1956, I started into the Moki Canyon ruins with a group of eight people. Everyone went up without difficulty and we spent several delightful hours poking through the ruins and look-

We always stop at Nankoweap along the Colorado in order to explore the prehistoric ruins.

ing at some petroglyphs. Then we started down. I had one passenger called Jack who apparently hadn't paid any attention to the height when he was climbing the wall. Neither had he thought much about it while scrambling in the ruins. When we started down however, he let out a wild scream. "How did I get up here? I'll never get down!"

"Oh, yes, you will," I told him. "Just turn around. Don't look. Go down like you came up."

But he could hardly move. He was trembling all over and his knees were shaking visibly. I sat down and studied the problem for awhile. I find that in a situ-

Though running downriver is often strenuous and exciting, there are moments on the trip that are just plain fun.

ation like this it doesn't pay to act in haste. In most cases if you consider the possibilities quietly you can often come up with a pretty good solution.

Finally, I got below Jack and with a lot of pleading, managed to work his feet into those first steps. That's how we went down. I would talk to him for awhile, then I would take hold of his foot and slowly work it down to the next step. Then I would quietly talk to him again.

That descent took almost two hours, but I got him down safely. It was then I realized that some people were going to have a lot of trouble with those heights and I would have to quit taking everyone up there. After that, I only took a select few up Moki Canyon to see the ruins. It's a shame too, because that was one of the most interesting sights in the Glen Canyon area.

Harry and I spent many days enlarging the Moki steps onto Rainbow Bridge. The bridge was a moderate seven-mile hike from the river, but very few people took this trip. Today Rainbow Bridge is a national monument and accessible over an easy one-mile trail from Lake Powell. As a result, thousands now visit it every spring and fall. The bridge itself is a fantastic sight. It's the greatest known natural bridge with a perfectly formed arch 309 feet above the stream bed and 278 feet wide. When I first hiked to the bridge, the access down was over tremendously tiny Moki steps and I could hardly put my toes in them. Harry and I spent hours there rubbing them with a large rock. When we finished, they were big enough to easily accommodate anyone who wanted to climb down. I even hammered in a piton and tied a rope to it so people would have something to hang onto.

In those days, I took hundreds of Scouts and others onto the bridge. Today, however, since it's in a national monument, the general public is no longer allowed to climb on the bridge itself and the Park Service has since removed the pitons.

The Scouts I used to take on the river loved this trip. There were a whole series of pools along the entire seven-mile route. I would hike them to the bridge and three miles beyond. Then I would let them swim their way down through the pools to the river. This was a total of twenty miles and qualified them for their twenty-mile hike. As far as most of them were concerned, this trip to Rainbow Bridge was the easiest twenty miles they had ever hiked.

One of my other favorites on the Glen was Smith Canyon, right on the river. The Indians here used the walls almost like a gigantic art gallery. The cliffs contained over 1000 petroglyphs. A few of the petroglyphs were very simple single drawings. Others were very complex panels. Some interpreters read elaborate legends into the placement of the figures and designs. I'm afraid I never tried to interpret what I saw but I enjoyed the variety. There were sheep in many forms, great serpents, spirals, open hands and flute players. Sometimes the flute player would be standing with a hump on his back, other times sitting and in a few cases, lying down. In addition, in Smith Canyon, I found pictures of hunters attacking sheep and Indians harvesting corn. Some people have told me that sheep represent hunting magic or a hunting adventure; serpents, meandering bends of a river; the hand, an oath of allegiance. I have never heard a satisfactory explanation for the flute player. Some say that it is a man seeking a wife; others say a legendary figure among the Indians. I never studied the petroglyphs from a scientific standpoint, but they were an enjoyable part of the river and the people I took with me always liked to see them.

Harry and I hiked to and enjoyed other areas during those years: Hidden Passage, Music Temple, Lake Canyon, Slick Rock and more. I think it's fair to say that there was a beauty and a uniqueness in those canyons that will never be duplicated anywhere else in the world. Today, all of that is under the water of Lake Powell. This, I think, is one of the crimes of modern bureaucracy. Most experts outside the government will tell you that dams have just about outlived their usefulness. They don't produce enough power to justify the tremendous expense, and the dams of the Southwest aren't really useful for diverting water for other purposes. The only reason they seem to exist is to keep the vast bureaucracy of the Bureau of Reclamation going and to provide a few outside jobs.

Like many other things, however, the pressure to build Glen Canyon Dam, and indeed, other dams on the Colorado River, was enormous. I opposed the dam vigorously and always urged anyone who came in contact with me to write his senators and congressmen in protest.

In many ways, I blame early environmental groups (the Sierra Club) for this fiasco. At the time the dam was in the planning stage, they didn't seem really very interested in the river. I think they used Glen Canyon Dam as a trade-off to keep a dam out of Dinosaur National Monument, Utah. Of course, this is only an opinion, but I do know that they expressed very little opposition and always urged me to temper my opposition. To me, this dam is a travesty for which we shall all pay forever.

Those early days on the Glen were, without a doubt, extremely pleasant ones. The Scouts that went with me on many trips loved being out in the canyon and they also loved the horseplay that went with it. I have to admit that during those years, so did I. I was always thinking up jokes to play on them. I made this into a sort of ritual at Hidden Passage. Hidden Passage is simply a passage between two canyons. Along the lower part were a number of pools where we could swim, then to get across to the other canyon, it was necessary to crawl on our elbows and toes along a ledge just slightly narrower than our bodies. Beyond that, we reached the top, the passage became steeper and narrower. The higher we climbed, the narrower it became. From below, it was impossible to see above until we popped out of the passage on top. On every trip, I would go first and take several dozen fresh eggs with me. Then as the boys came up, I would crack an egg on their heads. After several reached the top, they took great delight in cracking eggs on the heads of those below. It was like an initiation and the boys who had been there before always kept quiet so it would be a surprise to the others. They would laugh and shout and once everyone was up, they would kid each other about who looked the funniest. It was one of the highlights of the trip.

The fun and kidding that went on between myself and the Scouts seemed to prevail with the scoutmasters and other adults too. On these trips I always let the adults act as boatmen, but they were rather inexperienced and pretty rough on boats. As a result, they frequently sheered the pins in the outboard motors, by becoming tangled in the driftwood or hung on the rocks. We had a standing rule that if any boat sheered a pin, the other boats would come along and literally drown them with buckets of water. By this time, I had had so much experience and knew the area so well that I seldom had any trouble. While this wasn't a sore point between myself and the adults, it rather bruised their egos that a woman was better at it than a man.

On one particular trip as we approached Lee's Ferry, one of the scout leaders on my boat kept saying, "Georgie, how far to Lee's Ferry?"

"Why?" I asked.

"No reason; I just wondered." Then about half an hour later he'd ask again.

"Boy," I thought, "he's really anxious to get out of here this trip." Then suddenly I sheered a pin. I hadn't hit anything that I could see. I was in the middle of the channel away from all rocks and driftwood. I couldn't figure out what happened, when I turned to look at the scout leader he was grinning at me.

"Boy, am I glad that happened. I thought that pin would never let go."

Then he explained that all of them were getting so disgusted at sheering pins while I never did, that they decided to gang up on me. They had filed the pin in my motor almost in two. They were positive that I wouldn't go more than a couple

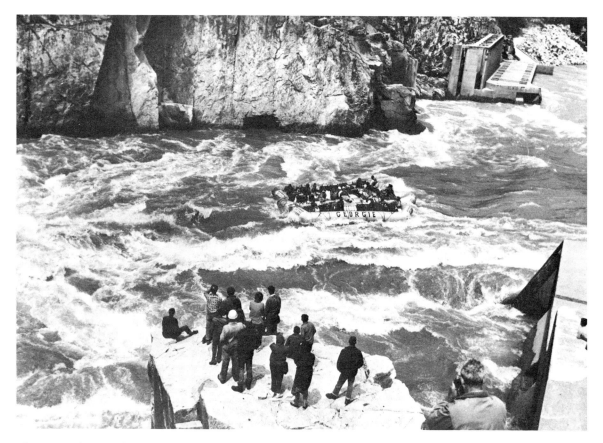

These are the rapids at Hell's Gate that we took on this trip without stopping. I make a practice of examining the different rapids frequently so that I know when their character changes.

of miles before it sheered all the way through. As it turned out however, I almost made it to Lee's Ferry. And the closer we got to Lee's Ferry, the scoutmaster told me, the more he began to sweat. "I knew we were out of food. And if that pin broke at the last minute and we couldn't put in there, we'd be swept right on down the canyon."

He was right, of course. In those days

we could go two or three weeks in the Grand Canyon without seeing another person, and once committed below Lee's Ferry, we couldn't come back. We'd have had to go all the way to Phantom Ranch before we could get additional supplies. It would have been a rather uncomfortable predicament. He was so glad to have that pin break that he pitched in to help me change it before the others caught up to throw water on us. We changed the pin in the record time of ten minutes and still beat them into Lee's Ferry. I'll never forget the look of relief on his face when that pin broke. While I thought he was just anxious to go home, he was just getting nervous about the possibility of being swept on down the canyon on an unscheduled trip.

I always found Glen Canyon to be one of my favorite trips. My main interest in running rivers of course, was to experience the rapids. There weren't many on Glen, but the scenery more than made up for this. Glen Canyon itself was completely isolated and miles and miles from the nearest civilization. During the 1950s there probably weren't more than four or five people in hundreds of square miles of desert. Sometimes I found it rather difficult to bring that point home to others. Everyone wanted to judge the Grand or Glen and other areas on the Colorado by their own standards. I've never really understood this. No matter how much experience or knowledge you have they still don't want to believe you. Sometimes even my own boatmen have to learn the facts the hard way.

On one particular trip in Glen, I had taken a German girl named Heidi who had gone on a number of kayak trips in Europe and expected the American experience to be similar to the European. In Europe, apparently, at night, the kayakers change their clothes and go to the villages to dance. The nearest village was at least two hundred miles away across some of the roughest, most rugged country in the United States. I thought I had made this clear in the very beginning.

After a day or two on one of these river trips, everybody begins to become pretty informal in his dress. I, for instance, wore one leopard-skin bathing suit the entire trip. Another girl wore ragged cut-offs. Most of the women let their hair go entirely and none wore lipstick. After all, it's hard to look your best when you're in the water all day and camping on a sandbar at night. We looked exactly like what we were: river rats out for a several-week trip on the river. About the third night I looked up and there stood Heidi dressed to the teeth. She was a fairly small dark girl and that night she looked terrific. Her hair was combed smooth, she had put on bright red lipstick and an electric blue dress. If I hadn't known better I would have sworn she was about to go out for a night on the town in Las Vegas. I must say, against the rugged river background, she looked really out of place.

"What's the occasion?" I asked her.

"Why I'm going to the village just like we did in Germany."

"Where did you get a crazy idea like that?" I asked her. "Even if you were to hike 125 miles across that desert country, you probably wouldn't find one other person let alone a whole village."

"It's right out there," she insisted. "It's got to be."

"This country just hasn't been settled as long as Europe," I said. "It's still pretty much frontier out here. Why, most of the roads aren't even paved yet. It's just different in the American West."

She shook her head, turned around and walked back towards the boat. When I saw her half an hour later she was again dressed like a typical river runner. Actually I'm not sure that I convinced her. She seemed determined to believe there was a village out there somewhere with a night-life. I, for some unknown reason, was trying to keep her from finding it.

During those years on Glen and Upper Colorado, life was never dull. Something unusual happened on nearly every trip. Not all of these experiences were exciting, of course, but some were unusual enough that they really stood out in my memory. On one occasion a movie company hired me to help make a movie called "Six Girls Against the Colorado." All of the girls were under eighteen so they asked me to play chaperone as well as run the boats. When they showed up at Hite, they looked like a traveling circus. They had brought six gorgeous Hollywood girls, an entire camera crew, and a number of other people to handle the miscellaneous functions. The first thing the director did after they un-loaded, was to pop down in his chair on the beach and order martinis. I remember watching him drink that martini and thinking, "Boy, this is going to be some trip."

We started out in Glen Canyon where they took a lot of general background scenes. Then they took the girls and a camera crew to Rainbow Bridge. Finally they began to photograph the dangerous scenes. The script called for the girls to overcome all sorts of hazardous experi-ences on the rugged Colorado. It was then I learned the real truth about motion pictures. Everything is fake. First they set girls up to take a fall from a high cliff. They took a long shot of one of the high cliffs. That set the scene. Iris McCollough, a tall, dark, buxom girl, handled many of the dangerous scenes. They had trouble

with Iris, however, because she had been a model for several years and always had difficulty remembering not to strike a static pose.

Next, they had Iris walk along the top of the cliff. Actually it was just a little spot outside camp. Next she fell and grabbed the top of the cliff. Next scene, the camera zoomed in to show her hanging hundreds of feet above the river. I almost died laughing over that one. They actually made that girl hang from the top of a little rock with her feet barely a foot above the ground. All she had to do was let go and drop easily to safety. They did a good job of creating an illusion, though, for in the finished movie it looked quite dangerous. It went on like this for the next few days while they filmed rattlesnakes, scorpions, girls falling into the water and a number of other hazards. All of it was fake.

After that we came downriver to Lee's Ferry to run the boat sequences and the upsets. Just below Lee's Ferry there is a small riffle with a few waves that can be made to look like a large rapid. Actually it doesn't amount to much and generally I go through this riffle without paying atten-tion. This trip, however, it was different. I was supposed to go through in a single boat and upset. Then I was supposed to show the girls in dangerous rough water. So I shot through the rapids, caught a wave just right and upset. I thought that would be that. But it turned out that they wanted to use different types of upsets throughout the picture. So I ran that same rapid over and over and over again. I never was so sick of anything in my life. I'd simply run through, do whatever they asked, put the raft on a truck, take it back to Lee's Ferry

Here I am with my trusty outboard and my trustier oar. It's necessary to use power to negotiate the rapids.

and start all over again. It got to be pretty boring after the tenth time.

They did a marvelous job of editing, though, and when the movie came out, they had interspersed bits of that rapid throughout the picture. It really looked like the girls were in trouble every inch of the way down the river. Not very authentic, but effective as far as the picture was concerned.

That was the only full length commercial film I ever helped make, but I did get in on several short films. First I was hired to help make the Disney short called "Grand Canyon." The crew for that twenty-one-day trip consisted of a director,

a cameraman, a Park Service ranger, his wife, myself and a boatman. To make pictures of the rapids, without excess motion, they installed some sort of a gyroscopic tripod on the front of my raft. With this they took some excellent pictures of the river. When it came time to photograph the logs and trees floating down the Colorado, they just couldn't seem to take the shots they wanted. Finally the photographer picked out a few small pieces of wood from the bank, threw these in the current and took his pictures. I understand they looked like the real thing on the screen. They also got some marvelous shots of mules crossing the bridge near Phantom Ranch, the burros, the lightning over the canyon. These were synchronized later with the music of the Grand Canyon Suite.

When we came to camp, I cooked for myself and my boatman. The ranger however, waited on that director hand and foot. He cooked, gathered wood, and even held the director over the bow of the boat while he took pictures. I didn't particularly enjoy this trip because I don't like people who expect special privileges like this. But I will admit, that finished picture turned out to be a work of art.

Fox and Paramount also made documentaries on the Colorado River, but these were an entirely different story. Both companies sent two men down the river with me to make their pictures. The cameras used on the river were large, shoulder-mounted 35 mm types. I felt extremely sorry for the cameramen who had to lug those big cameras over the rocks or carry them considerable distances to get the shots they needed.

The Paramount crew got excellent pictures. I was, however, disappointed in Fox. On Lava I made a special effort to make sure they got shots of the boats going through the hole. Instead of concentrating on the rapid, the cameraman got a perspective shot showing the boat and the top of the canyon. It showed the contrast, all right, but not good detail of the rapids. In general though the Fox photographer did a good job in the 95,000 cubic-feet-a-second water we had on that trip. Since his footage was supposed to show the entire canyon trip, the Fox photographer also wanted camp scenes such as people putting out their sleeping bags, fixing dinner and

similar shots. Every time I'd find a good one, I'd point it out and say, "Why not take that?"

Usually he was relaxing and chatting, so he'd say, "Tomorrow, Georgie. There is plenty of time." The last night came and he still didn't have any camp shots. Finally, in desperation, he just lined a few people up against a wall and shot the camp pictures. Later, in Chicago, I spotted a theatre running the Fox film so I got a number of river people together and we went to see it.

"Be quiet," I said, "and listen to what people say about this film."

They were saying, "Those people must be idiots . . . they're crazy . . . why would anyone do that?"

The picture, despite these comments, went over well and wound up being shown around the world. In my opinion, it did an overall excellent job of representing white water adventure as it really was.

As long as I'm talking about films, I might as well stop here and discuss two that I didn't make, but about which I have some strong opinions. The first is the Major John Wesley Powell expedition down the Colorado River called "Ten Who Dared." I believe strongly in making films of historic events. But in my opinion that film used history as a vehicle to tell a very warped version of the story. First, the company made the film in the studio, not on the river. That, to me, is unforgivable fraud. The only positive aspect was that they used the right kind of boats. But instead of showing the struggle the party had against nature and the river, they concentrated on the feuding that went on. In my opinion Powell told a terrific story, but the film really didn't depict the feat of running the river. It just showed the men fighting with each other.

A lot of people have asked me how I feel about the movie "Deliverance." I actually consider that film on a par with "Six Girls Against the Colorado." It was a fair story, but it wasn't authentic. All that was really seen of rapids there was a very small bit of film used over and over again. If a film is turned upside down, it looks like a different river. In "Deliverance," they made a small number of shots go an awfully long way. I really can't find fault with that technique of course, but when I see rapids, I like to see real ones. I guess I just can't get used to the methods used by Hollywood movie makers. The few movies I did help make were enjoyable and they taught me to look at movie making in an entirely different light.

One of the most unusual experiences I ever had on the Glen was my uranium prospecting trip. During the middle 1950s, the United States needed large quantities of uranium and there were indications that the Four Corners area of Utah, New Mexico, Colorado and Arizona contained huge deposits. As a result, prospectors from all over the country rushed to the area in a stampede that could well be compared to the California gold rush of 1849. Armed with Geiger counters, prospectors set out across the vast desert in search of uranium and instant wealth. As with most prospecting ventures, a few found uranium at the end of the rainbow, but most just got a lot of exercise for their effort.

At the height of this uranium craze in January 1955, I received a letter asking if I would be available to take a group of pros-

pectors on a month-long trip in Glen Canyon. The fee sounded good. My brother had been mining for years so I was familiar with prospecting and rather enjoyed it. I agreed to the idea and on April 15 I met a group of fifteen prospectors at Hite, Utah.

They had brought a huge mound of equipment with them, including Geiger counters, scintillation counters and other electronic gadgets. I took one look at all that stuff and wondered how I was going to get it in the big boat. I managed to stuff every last piece in somehow, and three hours later we shoved off.

My prospectors were all men in their thirties and forties and I learned as we went along that they all had a good knowledge of mining and geology. Their leader, a man called John, explained that they wanted me to stop wherever they asked. I could hike with them but I was not to take pictures of anyone or anything on this trip including the scenery. I agreed, and every morning we would start down the river, go a few miles, then stop at some designated spot where everyone would get out and explore.

Before coming on this trip, the group had signed up with a number of backers who had paid to have them go down the river for them and stake a claim. There was a lot of fraud at that time and some companies simply took the money and forgot to stake the claim. Not this one; they would search with their equipment until they found a pretty good vein of uranium, then they would give me a bucket of paint and I would paint the rocks around the area. After that, they would fill out the claim forms and have me sign as a witness. Later, they were filed to make it legal. Every one of those claims actually contained uranium. Today three-quarters of the claims are under water.

Every night, the men would sit around the campfire and tell tall tales of riches. I don't think I ever heard a figure under a million dollars the entire time we were together.

One day there was a lot of excitement about the next canyon downriver. When we pulled in, they divided into three groups and set off in different directions. I went along with the first party. No sooner had we scrambled into a side canyon than the scintillator went wild. I've never seen so much scrambling around. Finally, they drove stakes, marked the spot, made some notes, took a few rock samples and started back to the boat. When we got there we discovered that the two other parties had had almost the same experience. Everybody swore me to secrecy. I told them I didn't care how rich they got. All I wanted was to run the river in peace.

Three weeks later we pulled into Marble Canyon. The leader thanked me and they drove away in several cars that had been left for them. I never did know whether anything ever came of their big strike up in that canyon, but I had enjoyed the company and the experience. I had, once again, spent an entire month on the river and had the time of my life, so it was well worth it to me.

The coming of Glen Canyon Dam, of course, overshadowed everything on the Glen and Catarac Canyons from the late 1950s on. The Bureau of Reclamation first began to prepare the site in 1957 and on every trip I took through the canyon after

This is a lunch break on a river trip. The little wading pool is what we call a table.

that, I could see the progress. The site itself was quite isolated and the initial preparation took years. River running wasn't really affected too much until the 1960s when they began to divert the river around the dam base. From then on I could still come down most of the way. But just above the dam, I had to take the rafts out and truck them to Lee's Ferry.

Then in 1964 they completed the dam, an all-concrete affair which rises 710 feet from bed rock, and began to fill Lake Powell. We stopped going through Glen at that time, but since I knew it would take several years to fill the lower lake, we kept running Catarac Canyon for another two years. There probably isn't any water anywhere in the world quite like Catarac Canyon. For a day and a half, we ran through an area known as the big drop. The canyon walls were extremely steep here and unlike the Grand below, the water simply rushed on through the canyon without stopping. There was no backwater. When I reached the entrance to Catarac Canyon, I would have my people try swimming in life preservers. The chance of getting tossed out somewhere along the way was pretty good, and I wanted them to know something about the water. If they wanted to slow down, for instance, they brought their feet up; if they wanted to take off, they put them down. There were a few tricks I thought they needed to know and this seemed like a good place to practice.

Catarac was always different in different kinds of water, but it was especially fierce in high water. During the 1957 trip, for instance, there was a tremendous flow of water in Catarac, approximately 115,000 cubic feet per second. That's probably the biggest water I have ever seen there. The waves were just huge, some at least fifty feet high, and those thirty-foot pontoons of the big boat just stood on end. That river contained enormous holes which we fell into with a sickening thud. I couldn't believe it.

Sometimes the water became so bad on Catarac that people just panicked. On one trip, we ran well until we came to Satan's Gut, which is an extremely vicious rapid. The three-boat started out wrong and just literally bounced through the rapid. Below, it ran smack into a rock set out in midstream. At this point one of the

passengers became so terrified, he grabbed that rock and hung on for dear life. The first boat bounced off and went on with him still hanging there. There he was, clinging to a rock two feet above the raging water. The second boat managed to come in against the rock in spite of the fast water, but he wouldn't jump. Finally we put a rope on another fellow who jumped over and pried his hands off the rock and almost carried him hollering back to the boat. We then took him over to the big boat and gave him something to drink. When he left, he wanted to take his life preserver home because, as he told me, it had saved his life. It's always strange to me when people go into shock like that and I'm always amazed at the funny ideas they come up with. That life preserver had nothing to do with saving his life, but we couldn't tell him that.

I ran 1964 and 1965 without trouble. The water was now rising fast, but I thought that I'd be able to get in the Catarac Canyon run at least one more year. So in 1966 I started down from Green River, Utah, once again. We came through Labyrinth and Stillwater Canyons, and with me holding my breath, entered Catarac. For the first three hours, we shot through those rapids like we always had. Then suddenly we hit the backed-up water. The next rapid was almost under water, and the next, the big drop was completely gone. I pulled in and just stared at it. I had to admit I was extremely sad, but I decided to put off telling the rest of the party until next morning. They had been so hoping they would get in one last good run. But they were on to me. One girl who had been there before came over and said, "We're here at the big drop, aren't we Georgie? It's all over, isn't it?"

I nodded, and as the girl turned away to tell the others, the tears streaming down her cheeks. An era had come to an end.

Today, we don't run the upper canyon anymore. Some river runners run the Catarac and San Juan, but it's a float trip. I am, of course, still running the Grand Canyon. But the dams have really destroyed the entire Colorado adventure as I used to know it, and have changed the entire complexion of river running everywhere, forever.

The Navajo Experience

*I*t would be difficult to tell the story of river pioneering on the Colorado River without mentioning the Navajo Indians. In the first place, the Navajo reservation runs for many miles along both the San Juan and Colorado Rivers. In the early days I didn't know much about the Navajos although I would see them now and then on the river. I guess you might say that the Navajo experience grew on me as my life became more intertwined with the Colorado River itself and the surrounding desert country.

One of the first times I really became conscious of the Navajos and their ways was in the early days when Harry and I would take long desert hikes. On one trip we decided to repeat what was called the "Trail of the Fathers." In the early days a group of Mormons, looking for a new route, had started at Lee's Ferry, crossed the Colorado River at the "Crossing of the Fathers," then hiked out to Tuba City, Arizona.

Harry and I began this hike with overweight packs loaded down with canned food. When we reached the Crossing of the Fathers, we put some logs together just as the Mormons had, crossed the river and started up one of the side canyons.

From the bottom of the canyon we picked out the access that looked easy.

When we neared the top, however, it became obvious that we couldn't climb that final cliff. I admit that I was discouraged and tired since we had already climbed several thousand feet above the river. But I knew that there are many dead ends in the myriad of twisting side canyons. So I just shrugged my shoulders and headed back toward the bottom. Somehow, Harry and I became lost going back down and came out in the wrong canyon. Now we were in trouble. By the time we worked ourselves to the high desert beyond, we had lost several days, and almost depleted our food supply. Sixty miles from our destination we ate our last can of tomatoes. I was really apprehensive. I had heard horror stories of people losing their strength when they ran out of food, but surprisingly, that didn't happen to us. In the next few days we found we were mentally sharper and hiked much better than before. Curiously, the buzzards began to circle low over us. I said to Harry, "Are you sure you have to stop moving before they come to get you?"

Finally, after three days of this, we came to a place called Rainbow Trading Post. I don't remember being particularly happy to see it since, at this point, I was not terribly hungry or tired.

The post was closed but under a nearby shelter we began talking to a Navajo Indian sitting there who could speak a little English. I had heard that Indians went without food for days when they hunted their sheep. Now I was curious, so I asked how long they could really go.

He shrugged his shoulders and said, "Seven days." I really thought he was kidding, but I later found he was serious

and actually the Indians sometimes went much longer than this.

Within a short time the trader came home, and we bought some candy bars and began to eat one every three hours so we wouldn't get sugar too fast on an empty stomach.

The memory of what that Navajo told us about going seven days without food kept haunting me for a long time after that. I had thought at that time that going three days without food was quite a feat, but to go seven, eight or nine days really impressed me. After all, no white man I knew could do anything like that.

After that episode, I didn't see many Indians for some time. The Navajos are a very shy people. Hiking in Glen Canyon, we would come upon sheep grazing but we seldom saw an Indian with them. Since sheep on the Navajo reservation were always accompanied by an Indian attendant, we knew he had seen us coming well in advance and hid.

It was indeed a rarity when a Navajo would let us see him. One time hiking to Navajo Mountain, one fellow stood his ground and let us come to him. He couldn't speak much English but we managed to make him understand that we wanted to know how much further it was to Navajo Mountain. At that time, they often traveled in a wagon with big wheels and measured distance with the wagon. The Indian nodded that he understood. He took his hand and made a big arc from the ground on one side of his body to the ground on the other side. This meant we had one more day to travel.

As I began to make river trips on the San Juan and had to cross their reservation by truck, I began to see them more often. I also kept hearing intriguing tales about the life they led. The Navajos had a matriarchal society: the woman always kept her name; the sheep automatically passed to her; and she could divorce her husband by merely putting his things outside the hogan. A hogan is a Navajo mud house which always faces East and resembles an upside-down bowl. Although some were made partially of wood, most were mud with dirt floors. Many of the Navajos, even in the late 1950s, couldn't speak English and the older ones talked with a deep-in-throat rumble that most people couldn't understand.

I also kept hearing tales about an unusual missionary by the name of Shine Smith who lived with the Indians. All of this fascinated me so much that when I heard that Shine Smith was giving a Christmas party for the Navajos near the Cameron Trading Post, I decided to go see for myself.

I saw, all right, and what I saw really opened my eyes. Almost two thousand Indians came to that party. Most of them didn't own cars or trucks and had come in from the remote parts of the reservation by wagon. It had snowed the night before and a cold chilling wind was blowing across the desert. Shine set up some makeshift tables just out in the open to hold the food and blankets he had managed to obtain. The Indians formed a long line and Shine was everywhere at once helping to give out the little food he had. I don't think even a quarter of the Indians got food before he ran out. That really bothered me. But I didn't hear one single complaint and no one shoved or shouted. They just smiled and seemed grateful for what Shine was doing.

Although wood is extremely scarce on the reservation, some of the Indians hiked up a nearby mountain and brought back a huge quantity of firewood. They built a number of fires, and after Shine passed out what food he had collected, the women cut up meat, potatoes, celery and other vegetables into a big tin washtub and cooked one of the most delicious stews I have ever tasted. They also made a cornmeal-baking soda mix they called squaw bread, which they deep-fried in a pan over the fire.

These parties, of course, were enough reason for a day-long feast. Family groups would usually cook together, but the Indians would also wander from group to group talking to everybody.

That was one experience that profoundly affected me that day. The other was meeting Shine Smith. Shine was one of those big, rough-and-ready types with grey hair and a husky booming voice that always made people notice him. The Presbyterian Church originally sent him to the Navajo reservation to establish a religious center. The Indians, however, lived scattered across this huge reservation. Shine took one look at the plight of these people and decided that if he were going to be of real help, he must get out on that reservation and go to them. This was exactly what the Indians needed. He nursed them when they got sick and helped deliver their babies. When he found Indian families without food, he made sure they got some. He learned the Navajo ways and went all over the reservation helping where he could. Sometimes they needed him at the oddest moments.

In one case, Shine was riding across the reservation on a horse when he came across a Navajo boy running at top speed across the desert.

"My mother is having a baby," he told Shine in Navajo. "Come quick."

So Shine lifted the boy up on the horse with him and rode eight miles back across the desert to a lone hogan sitting on a hill. Inside, Shine found an almost delirious Navajo woman in labor. A half hour later, with Shine's assistance, she gave birth to a baby girl. Her temperature seemed so high that Shine wondered if she'd make it through the night. He managed to give her some antibiotics which he always carried for such emergencies. Sometime during the night, her fever broke and by next morning she could talk. She told Shine in Navajo that she was living alone with two children. She had been so sick she was afraid her baby would die. So she sent the two kids in different directions for help. About noon, several Navajos showed up, but by this time, both mother and baby were doing fine.

Another time, coming across the reservation, Shine discovered a family that hadn't eaten for at least two weeks and had been chewing cactus to stay alive. This time, he rode for two days across the desert to a food supply cache he kept for this purpose and came back with enough food to keep them going for several months. As a result, the Indians loved and trusted him.

Despite efforts like this, however, he and the church parted ways. The problem was that they wanted to establish a central church building and Shine refused. In my opinion, bureaucracy and politics should never be allowed to stand in the way of

This is my good friend, Shine Smith, who spent a large part of his life serving as a minister on the Navajo reservation.

getting the job done. I guess I'm pretty naive but I always thought the Christian way was to provide whatever people needed when they needed it. In this case, they could have accomplished so much by supporting Shine financially. As it was, he did what he could, but he just never had enough money to go around.

When I asked him at the time about the lack of food at Christmas he said, "I tried, Georgie, but I couldn't get any more."

Besides meeting Shine Smith at that Navajo Christmas party, I also met the famous Arizona Highways photographer, Joseph Muench. That meeting also affected my life greatly because over the years Joe and I have become great friends. He has gone with me many times on the river. And since he takes many "Thru-The-Lens" club tours around the world, he has helped greatly by scouting out likely rivers for exploration in Alaska, Canada and other remote spots.

When I left the reservation that day, I was determined to take matters into my own hands and see what I could do to make the next year's party a success. Once back in Los Angeles I really swung into action. In Los Angeles they have a giant market complex where the retail food stores come to buy produce. I first went to the general manager of the market.

"I'm Georgie White," I told him. "I know sometimes you have produce left over. I need any surplus you might have for the starving Navajos. Can you help?"

I guess I must have impressed him with my determination for he said, "Georgie, this market is made up of a lot of distributors. You'll have to ask them individually, but I'll recommend that they help. I'll do all I can to help you obtain the food you need."

Later I talked to dozens of individuals, most of whom said that they would be delighted to donate produce. All in all, it looked like I would collect tons of celery, watermelon, carrots and many other fruits and vegetables. I also called dozens of newspapers, radio and television stations and asked them to print or broadcast an appeal for food and clothing for the Indians. As a result, I received hundreds of calls and spent weekends driving around gathering up bundles that people donated. Then I came home and set up a separation

counter in my back yard. I had asked for low-heeled shoes and warm clothing, but they gave me just about everything. So I separated out the high-heel shoes and fancy clothing and donated these to the Salvation Army. By fall of that year, I had literally collected tons of food and clothing.

What I needed next was some way to get it to the reservation. I had appealed for a truck in the radio and television announcements and from these I received a few phone calls. I also started making the rounds of trucking companies.

"I have tons of food for the Navajos," I told them. "I need trucks at Christmas to get the food to the reservation."

Most of the companies turned me down but a few said they might help later. One agreed to donate a truck if I would drive it. And that's what I did. Christmas Eve afternoon, I backed a huge shining silver trailer truck into the produce market and with the help of a dozen men, loaded it full of surplus produce. When we finished I don't think I could have stuffed one more head of lettuce into that trailer.

When I worked my way out of downtown traffic and headed out for Cameron, Arizona that afternoon, I really felt good. There had been times during the year when I had become terribly discouraged, but that was behind me now. The Indians were going to have a real celebration.

I had driven many different types of trucks for many years, so driving a huge trailer didn't seem at all out of the ordinary. After about an hour, everything became routine. Eight hours later I pulled into Cameron Trading Post, five hundred miles from Los Angeles. The Indians went wild. They loved the fresh celery and other vegetables.

"Georgie," Shine told me, "this is the best party we have ever had. I don't know how you got so much food."

"Wait until next year" I told him, "we'll have even more."

After that I really got organized. I needed people to help drive the trucks and distribute food at the party. So I called one of the Los Angeles breweries that I knew would provide free beer and invited all my friends to a party. There I showed pictures of the Navajos and asked everyone to help. As a result, I had all the volunteers I needed for next Christmas.

At that time, I had started working again during the winter as a security guard at Douglas Aircraft. On the job, I appealed to the workers to help the Indians. Douglas itself, gave a few blue security suits and jackets. The Navajo men loved these. In addition, other Douglas people gave me tons of food and money—and some of the men came out to Arizona to help with the party.

I started asking almost everyone I knew to donate something. Sometimes, the results were rather startling. The Navajo women loved those old treadle sewing machines for making clothes. One of the women who went down the river with me regularly, Helen Kendall, decided to start collecting sewing machines around Los Angeles area. Helen was somewhat eccentric and rode around the city on a motorcycle equipped with a sidecar. Frequently she would show up at my house carrying a treadle sewing machine in the sidecar for me to take out to the Navajos.

Responses like these always made me feel especially good.

After I accumulated all of those items, I went back to the truck companies. Many more agreed to provide trucks that next year and a few gave me a free driver as well. I liked this best because then the driver would come back and tell about seeing the Indians mixing their bread and stew.

The Navajo truck line proved especially helpful. Over the years they hauled large quantities of freight to Flagstaff, Arizona, absolutely free. I'm not sure it's possible to put a dollar value on what they did, because at times without their help, tons of food would have spoiled.

After about the third year, I decided that the Navajo children needed a Santa Claus. Of course, Santa Claus wouldn't have the same meaning to them that it did to us, but I felt sure they would enjoy the idea anyway. That November I bought a bright red Santa Claus suit and tried to get some of my male friends to wear it, but they refused. So that Christmas, I dressed up in the suit, stuffed a couple of pillows in my stomach, and passed out candy and toys. I didn't fool those kids one bit. They would simply laugh and point at my boots, then they would pet the suit and pull on the whiskers. They loved it. Whenever I wore that suit, I always had a group of noisy Navajo kids following me.

This was always enjoyable, but I think the biggest thrill I received in those days as far as the children were concerned, came from the "Queen for a Day" television show. I wrote and said if they made me a queen for a day, I would want a ton

I used to dress up like Santa for the little children on the reservation, though I wonder if I really had them fooled.

of candy for the Navajo children.

I didn't hear for some time, so I forgot it. Then one day, the show called and said that that wasn't exactly their line but to come in anyway and they would arrange something. On the show, they let me tell my story and asked for applause. On the meter, I received more applause than anyone else, but because they generally give away furniture, they gave me second place. Then after the show, they gave a ton of candy to the children.

After Shine's Christmas parties ended, I found that some of the Indians didn't have any way to get back to their homes unless they walked. So I would usually drive a family or two out over the reservation to their hogan. The Navajo reservation is big and empty and I didn't really know it too well. At that time, all the desert looked the same to me. Generally, the Indians would tell me how to get to their hogans but then I had to come back on my own.

One time, I drove out over a narrow one-track desert road for at least fifty miles to drop off one family and when I started to return, the snow had completely covered my tracks. I'll never forget that Indian standing there pointing out the distance toward the highway.

I started off slowly in that direction. Before I had gone two miles, I became stuck in the snow. So I took the planks out of the back of my pickup that I carried for my San Juan trips and dug myself out. Finally, I reached the highway, which didn't mean that much because, at certain times of the year, you could drive a hundred miles without seeing another car. As a result, I always carried a sleeping bag so if I broke down, I could at least camp somewhere along the highway until help came or I figured out a way to help myself.

Those were good days. I was, however, appalled at the plight of the Indians. Food was very hard to come by on the reservation and most of the Indians didn't really have the basic necessities of life.

After meeting the Navajos at Shine's party, I became better and better acquainted with some individual families. Finally, they began to invite me to their hogans. I became quite close to some of them. One of the women I used to take food to had a blind baby. At first, the authorities felt they could help, so they took the child to the hospital in Utah. It turned out that they couldn't do anything so they returned the child to the mother.

Next Christmas when I stopped to visit, I found this baby crawling around in freezing temperatures without any clothes on. I climbed right back in my pickup, drove to Flagstaff before the stores closed and bought some clothes, then came back and dressed the baby. The next time I saw the mother, she didn't have the baby and somebody had put up a cross outside the hogan. She wouldn't talk about it but I'm sure the baby was buried there in the front yard. I had hoped the child would be all right, but life was tough on the reservations and often families just didn't have the basic needs for a minimum existence.

One of the Navajo men, Frank Black, worked for me on the river for several years, helping to rig the boats. Frank wasn't a big man but he was extremely strong. He had lost an eye in a mining accident several years before and he always wore something like a handkerchief over one eye. He pulled so hard on the ropes when he lashed my boats that I was afraid he would pull the boats in two. He spoke only broken English so I always used sign language and my own version of pidgin English to make him understand that I wanted him to take it easy. I would say, "don't-cut-the-boat-in-two." He used to think that was funny and nod so I knew he understood.

After I had known him for several years, I decided that maybe it would be fun to spend a winter in one of the hogans with Frank's family to see what it was like. I got a lesson out of that one.

It was very cold on the reservation. As a result, the kids sleep near the door of the hogan while the older people occupy positions in the back out of the draft, sleeping with feet toward the middle and shoulders to the outside. That first night I almost froze to death and after a few days, I simply gave up and moved back to Los Angeles.

I did become extremely good friends with many of the Navajo families. I think one of the reasons that I enjoyed the Indians so much was that their philosophy matched mine very closely. For one thing, they didn't yell at their children. Often at Christmas parties I would see dozens of children playing but I never heard parents raise their voices to them. The Navajos were neither grabby nor pushy. I have seen them stand in line for hours without shoving each other or trying to crowd in. And when it came their turn to take food, they took only their share. This was in

sharp contrast to some other people I observed. In addition, they never littered. They used every piece of paper or can; we never found any on the desert. They didn't believe in killing anything. They never hurt a rattlesnake or an insect and they wouldn't fish. This matched my views perfectly. I have always believed that we should leave nature as we found it. I have never touched anything on the river. Even when I have found saddles, pottery or oars or anything else, I have left them for others to see and enjoy. On my trips I always make sure no one harms the animals, including the rattlesnakes and the scorpions.

Although I could never live on the reservations as the Navajos did, I found many things about their lives that I really enjoyed. The Navajos truly lived in harmony with themselves and with nature and that's a lesson I feel the rest of us should learn.

After I became acquainted with Shine and the Navajos, when I was running the river on a regular trip, Shine would show up on the bank and bless my trip. The last time I remember this happening was early in the summer of 1957.

At Lee's Ferry just as I was about to pull out on a trip through the canyon, Shine Smith and three old Navajos appeared on the bank. The oldest, a "singer" as the Navajos called their medicine men, blessed the trip by strewing a pinch of cornmeal on the breeze and prayed for the happy completion of my journey. Things like this I shall never forget.

After the dam construction, Shine Smith died, and things began to change.

I felt very lost during that time. The Navajos took jobs at the dam construction site, and others began to move away from the reservation and drop the Navajo ways. There was talk of oil being discovered on the reservation and of course, uranium mining brought many outsiders.

There are no more Christmas parties on the reservation now, but I shall never forget those years. They were just as much a part of my learning about the Colorado River as running the rapids.

Coming of Age on the River

*T*hose middle years were really full of crisis for me. I was, by this time, absolutely obsessed with the idea of sharing the river experience with everyone. Not only did I want to open the rapids to people who were naturally adventurous and had the physical stamina for rough white water, I wanted to make the river accessible to everyone regardless of age, sex or physical condition.

That was the dream, but the reality was that during my pioneering years I could hardly get anyone to go with me. At this point I began to realize that if I were to succeed in popularizing this sport I must somehow take the river story to millions of people, not the few hundred I had been able to reach so far.

One of my first efforts in this direction was to try to get the nearby newspapers to give me extensive coverage. This effort met with mixed results. Years before I had gotten tremendous headlines when the papers thought Harry and I had drowned in the Grand Canyon, but to convince them to publicize the fact that a woman was running the rapids successfully when very few men could do it, seemed to be a different story. I called several large Southern California newspapers to see if they would give me coverage. They were extremely evasive. I had one reporter tell me to my face that if I were a man a lot of people would be interested. But since I was a woman he just wouldn't run the story.

In another case, a prominent Los Angeles newspaper man hiked in to Lava Falls, at my insistence, to report on river running on the Colorado River. His story, when it came out, told about running the river in wooden boats and how they had to take these boats out and portage the big rapids. Finally in a short side statement he said, in effect: "Oh yes, Georgie White is there running the rapids." He could have done so much for me if he had told the whole story about my running the rapids safely in large rafts, but he didn't. Despite the fact that I was then the only one on the river able to run rafts through the rapids without portaging, he completely ignored it.

Finally, Laura Bell, a reporter from the Boulder City newspaper began to get interested in what was happening on the Colorado River. She came out, interviewed me, took a number of pictures and gave me some excellent write-ups. This helped. Later, however, she told me that the publisher had expressed some objections about giving me publicity. I have to admit it was discouraging. Not only did this attitude extend to newspapers but even the general public didn't seem to want to hear about running rapids. I can remember one example quite clearly.

I was flying east from Los Angeles over the Grand Canyon on a commercial airliner. As we approached the canyon I stared intently at the river trying to make out some of the rapids. After watching me for a few minutes the woman in the seat beside me said, "You seem really interested in the Grand Canyon. Have you ever been there?"

"Yes," I said, "I run a raft through the rapids on the river down there every chance I get."

At that, she turned her back and didn't say another word the entire trip. I know it seems strange, but for some reason that seemed to typify the attitude in those days.

At this point I think I would have tried almost anything. I knew I needed greater publicity about the river. I just didn't know how to go about getting it. Obviously newspapers were not the right source.

Then I received a phone call from a photographer named John Goddard. He was, he told me, a photographer-lecturer who put on hundreds of lectures every year before such groups as Kiwanis, Lions, other clubs and churches. Some of his pictures also ran on national television. He said he would like a free trip on the river with me in return for the publicity.

Boy, did I jump at that! Goddard seemed like the answer to my prayers. By introducing my river trips to thousands of professional people he could do me a tremendous amount of good. This was the break I had been waiting for.

Goddard came on the trip, went on all the hikes, took pictures through the rapids and spent a great deal of time talking to everyone. When we reached Boulder City, he left to put his lecture tour together.

I waited expectantly. But when he began lecturing I was bitterly disappointed.

I had hoped Goddard would show the river as it was: people of all ages running the rapids safely; good fun in camp; and the beautiful scenery of the Colorado River country. Unknown to me, however, Goddard didn't have anything at all like that in mind.

He had brought along a rubber scorpion on a string and had somebody take pictures while he pulled it along on his sleeping bag. He avoided taking pictures of either women or children on the trip. He showed the men in only the most heroic scenes: running the more dangerous rapids; climbing high above the river; lowering themselves down a cliff and similar breathtaking action. He told everyone that he had been bitten by a rattlesnake and that he had battled danger every inch of the way. In short he scared the pants off anyone who saw his pictures. I was so angry I could have killed him on the spot. Every time he gave that lecture he did me irreparable harm. I had hoped for honest publicity and he was going around the country telling a pack of lies.

Back in Los Angeles I used to watch for the announcement of his lectures in the newspapers, and then attend them. Just my presence, in many cases, made him tone down the untruths. Goddard played the church circuit and sometimes the things that happened there amazed me. He always gave the impression that he had simply taken a few of his friends through the Grand Canyon. In one case I came in to hear the preacher say, ". . . and let us pray for our friend who braved the dangers of the Colorado River and brought his friends through safely." That was almost too much for me. At that same lecture Goddard told about being bitten by a rattlesnake. Apparently he hadn't seen me

in the audience. Afterwards I came up to him and said, "Let's hear that snake story again." He turned beet-red and didn't say a word.

I never confronted him in front of an audience but my presence always disturbed him. Finally I said, "If you aren't going to tell the truth at least pay me for the passage, then you can say what you want." A short time later, that is exactly what he did.

Unfortunately, what Goddard did wasn't terribly unusual. For some reason I had a lot of people go with me at that time who wanted to sensationalize and to present the worst side of the trip. I had a doctor friend, for instance, who insisted on showing only the roughest examples back home. He showed only the sand blowing, the dirty water, the hardships. When I asked him why, he said flatly, "I don't want other people going on the canyon. I want pictures that nobody else has. If everybody goes then I won't be doing anything different."

What a blow! I had been working for years to open the river to everyone. I had spent thousands of dollars of my own money and literally thrown my entire life into it. But every time I tried to put the real river story out and attract people, I was thwarted. I'm afraid at that point I had almost resigned myself to the fact that river adventure would never become popular and that I would never be able to attract large numbers of people to go with me.

That was without a doubt the low point of my career. Then something happened that gave me tremendous hope. That

Christmas I received in the mail, a letter and a package from Walter Baylock, a friend of Goddard who had gone with me down the river, and who owned a camera shop in Twin Falls, Idaho.

"I hate what Goddard is doing," the letter said, "but you will never get the story out until you take your own pictures and get them on television. Here is a 16 mm camera. Take pictures with it next season and good luck."

What a break. Unless you have been in the state of poverty that I was in at that time you will never realize what that gift meant. I had put every penny I made into rafts, equipment and supplies. I just barely had enough money left to eat. I could in no way afford that kind of a camera, so it meant the world to me. It was a ray of hope. Up to that point I hadn't been quite sure what path I should take to get the publicity I needed to call attention to the river adventure. Now it became crystal clear.

Next season I became a camera fanatic. I shot pictures of everything: rapids, cooking meals, campfire, hiking, swimming, air mattress floats and even water fights. I was determined to show all the good things. I was an amateur photographer, however, so a lot of what I shot came out underexposed, shaky, and without good subject matter. But I also took a lot of good pictures.

Now, of course, I had the problem of getting them on television. The fellow who had given me the camera said, "I know it's going to be hard to crack TV, Georgie. But you live in the Los Angeles area where many of them are produced;

you have exciting pictures and you aren't bashful. So start knocking on doors. Just make a pest of yourself until somebody gives in."

That's exactly what I did. I think I called everyone who had anything at all to do with TV. I didn't know a thing about agents in those days and I still don't. I just kept calling. Sometimes the TV producers wouldn't talk to me. Other times they'd say they just weren't interested.

Then Goddard got his film on the Jack Douglas show, "Bold Venture." There were all those lies again. He showed the scorpion crawling up the sleeping bag. He told how rough it was on the river. He wound up by saying only the most adventurous could go. I was so mad I could have spit. I called and arranged for an appointment with Jack Douglas. I said to him, "You say you tell the truth on your program. But most of what you showed were lies."

"I'm just starting out," I told him. "I can easily take older people and young children on my big raft in complete safety. But the way you told it who would believe this? Being a woman, how on earth will I get people of all ages to go if you keep putting out false information?"

"Look," he said, "I'm just starting too." And he was. He had a very small staff and a small sparsely furnished one-room office with a single gas heater.

"I'll get your film on somehow. Even if it is rough I will run it for you. You won't get paid, but at least you'll get the publicity."

I still had all my film completely unedited, but I just brought it all in and plunked it down on his desk. Jack cut out the bad shots and put it in some order. I had gotten lucky on that first try and came up with some terrific shots. One showed a spectacular lightning storm over the canyon. Others showed some unusually good rapid sequences. Those pictures brought the true river adventure story to hundreds of thousands of people for the very first time.

Jack asked me questions and I corrected everything Goddard had said. "Being a photographer," I said, "Goddard had to exaggerate. We seldom see snakes. We didn't have any scorpion bites that trip. We take older people, women, children. Everybody can enjoy the trip in complete safety."

Next, I managed to get myself on the Art Linkletter show. I arranged this by calling his producer, or as Art called her, his "girl Friday." She was a young lady about my size and we got along famously. The day of the show she and I were sitting in the office chatting when Art walked in.

He hadn't met me before and he just stared. "You're Georgie?"

Somehow in his mind he had decided that anyone running rapids had to be big and muscular like a football player. "Why you're no bigger than my producer here. Gee, you're not what I expected at all."

He kept looking at me and saying, "You're not what I expected." Finally, I guess he decided I was the real Georgie. He then explained I had just one minute of show-time. That was all right with me. I'm a non-stop entertaining talker. Give me a minute and I can usually expand on it. That's what I did on the Art Linkletter Show.

Art showed a few film clips then he asked questions: "Georgie, tell me, aren't you ever afraid?"

"Yes I'm afraid, but not on the river. I feel water is my friend. But when I get on the freeway and someone else is driving then I'm scared to death."

That broke him up.

That show, of course, really helped. I received many comments and much attention from that appearance. People were now beginning to learn about the river. I couldn't have been more delighted. After that I appeared on the Art Linkletter show every year for many years.

Next came a program with a well known comedian (who will remain nameless) famous for his put down humor. In many ways I'm sorry that I ever went on that program. This particular comedian used what I would call exploitive humor. This is the first show I had ever gone on where they gave the questions and expected me to go over them and work up the answers.

They wanted me to talk about sex on the river. "The river is for adventure," I said. "No way am I going to talk about sex."

"If you insist on talking about something sensational, then let's talk about Mexico. I'll play up the fact that there are alligators there, that they have snakes in the trees, and that the jungles are full of large, horrible bugs."

Well that seemed to be all right. "Now," his man Friday said, "you have to play up to our host because he's the one that is supposed to get the laughs. Remember that."

So on the show he did talk about

Mexico. He got laughs out of the snakes and the alligators and the mosquitoes. He really put river rafting down.

Several weeks before, I had run Catarac Canyon and the body of an adventurer who had drowned in a rapid bumped against my boat. Since the body was in an advance state of decomposition we pushed it over to shore with the oars, dug a hole up on a hillside and buried it. A Catholic priest on the trip then said the last rites.

So the host continued to flip cutting comments at me: "You know Georgie, with all those horrible things that happen on the river and the problems you have, what you really need on your trips is an undertaker."

My mind went blank. All I could think of was that body, and burying it in the sand. "Oh no," I said almost unconsciously, "you don't need an undertaker. You just take a shovel along and bury all bodies right there on the spot." That broke up the audience.

He just stood there and stared at me. After another couple of questions he shuttled me off stage. Later I heard that he was quite unhappy that I got that laugh. On his program this particular comedian apparently was supposed to get all the laughs.

Actually I was sorry I had made that statement about dead bodies. It was terrible publicity. After all, who was going to come on the river if they thought there was a chance that they would be buried on the spot? If I had ever been offered another chance to go on that show again, I can assure you that I would have turned it down.

In later years I also appeared on the

Here's a photo of me from my album—one winter when I was away from the river.

"To Tell The Truth" television show. On this show a panel of four celebrities, Polly Bergen, Bill Cullen and two others had to guess who the real "Georgie" was from among three different people. Since I am so small, however, and really don't look much like a river adventurer I managed to fool everyone but Bill Cullen who pointed to me and said, "She has to be the real 'Georgie'; she is the only one that came down the steps without looking or holding the handrail. I'm sure that's the kind of self-confidence it takes to run a raft through the rapids."

Along with these television experiences I also started going to the San Francisco boat show in the late 1950s. I simply brought the big boat up from Los Angeles by truck, blew the twenty-five by thirty-five foot raft up with a hand pump and put it inside a booth. In the beginning, that huge raft was a novelty so I stopped the show. The first time I appeared I attracted a tremendous crowd.

At first, however, I really worried about my raft. Young boys would come by and kick the boat. Then they would loosen the oar locks. Finally they would say things about what a pocket knife could do to it.

I got so worried I practically sat up all night to guard that boat. After all it was the only boat I had, and I just didn't have the cash to replace it.

Several years later I added the Chicago boat show and later with the help of my boatmen, the Los Angeles show, that takes place in Anaheim.

At the shows I always run movies of river rafting. Unfortunately, I always have trouble deciding just what kinds of pictures to show. If I show too many camp scenes, people just walk on by. If I show big rapids, they stop, but they say, "That looks too dangerous." "You'll never get me to go on one of those trips." "No way."

I have never been sure those shows were effective in reaching the type of people who run the river. But a lot of people see boat shows every year so I suppose every little bit of exposure is helpful.

Within a few years I had appeared on many television shows. My movies of the North Country (Alaska and Canada), Mexico and the Colorado River had been

shown all across the United States and in many foreign countries. As a result of this more and more people began to write and to take river trips with me. I hcard from families who wanted to take children. I told them to come ahead. I heard from women in their sixties and seventies who wondered if they could make it. These people I encouraged too.

As time went on, the size of my trips became larger and larger until it wasn't at all unusual for me to leave Lee's Ferry, Arizona with two sections of forty people each.

After that I really stopped being just a river runner and became a commercial operator and trip leader, jobs that require far different skills from the ones I had been using up until this time. Large groups of people, of course, always present special problems, but in a wilderness setting like the Colorado River those problems often become intensified.

At this point I had to provide boatmen to run the two sets of little boats. I had to provide for the safety of from forty to eighty people. I had to provide food for up to thirty days on the river, and finally I had to make sure each and every group really enjoyed the trip. Faced with these same tasks, other operators have decided that taking large groups on the river just wasn't worth it. I can truthfully say that it is worth it for me and that I have enjoyed every minute of it.

I think the saving grace for me is that deep down I'm a "people person." Despite the fact that I've spent a great deal of time alone on the river I like to study all types of people. Often when I'm on a river trip I'll look terribly involved in patching or pumping a boat, or in doing some other necessary chore, and of course, I am. But I'm also watching the people. I like to see how they react to each other and to their surroundings.

Often when I meet someone before a trip I'll unconsciously try to decide how they will react on the river. It surprises me just how hard it is to judge. The river is a great tester. Those I expect to do well quite often don't, and those I expect to have trouble often have the time of their lives. You might say, though, that I always find this human drama terribly exciting.

When I started to master the art of running rivers with large groups of people, the first problem I faced was that of getting just the right boatmen for my kind of trip. This sounds simple, but it took me a number of years. The boatman problem, of course, actually started with the early ten-man rafts. When we load a raft of that size with enough supplies for a twenty-one to thirty-day trip, we can only take three to four passengers per boat along with someone to row it. My brother Paul by that time had become quite proficient at running rapids, so he would often handle a second boat. When he didn't, I had to find someone else who was good enough to make this trip safely.

To solve this problem I began to train others. My first boatmen were simply adventurous people who could handle a ten-man raft. In those early days on the Colorado River, no one really knew how to run the huge rapids very well. Nevills had been running them for some time in wooden boats and he was quite expert, but there were very few others who could do it well.

By this time I had more experience on the Colorado River than anyone else and I was beginning to feel quite competent on all rapids. As a result, I decided that although others could row in the calm water and the miscellaneous rapids, I must take the responsibility and row every major rapid myself in every boat. That might sound difficult, but here's how it worked: First, I would run the rapid in my own boat, and land. Then I would walk back to where the next boat was waiting and I would run it through. This worked well except for one major flaw.

One afternoon I ran a particularly bad rapid, landed and walked back to bring the next boat through. Halfway down, a wave caught the boat, tipped it up on a forty-five degree angle, spun us halfway around, then shot us violently through the rapid. As I came out on the bottom I glanced toward the shore to see four very nervous passengers watching the action with great apprehension.

For a minute I didn't understand their concern, then suddenly it dawned on me. I was courting disaster. What if I should get swept downstream and be unable to return because of the current and the impassibility of the canyon? Those people on the bank would be stranded. It would be almost suicide for them to run the rapids by themselves. And in most cases they couldn't walk out since there are few escape routes along the entire 280 miles of canyon.

At that time I couldn't stop running the boats myself because I didn't have enough experienced boatmen available. But after that I did become extremely cautious.

Until I developed the three-boat and

the big boat I didn't use many boatmen. But after 1955 I started running with the big boat and one or two of the three-boats. Since I could then only handle the big boat myself, I had to rely on boatmen to bring the small boats downriver.

I solved this problem partially by recruiting people who knew the river reasonably well and had some experience. The three-boats, of course, were extremely awkward and rowing them was a problem. Two boatmen had to sit fourteen feet apart and work together as a team. The timing must be perfect so that just the right amount of pressure is exerted at the right time. Too much pressure in a rapid and you are in the hole on one side, too much on the other and you're in the hole on that side. Invariably my trainee boatmen during those years would try to compete with each other, give their strokes tremendous pressure and wind up in one of the holes. I tried to talk them out of this extreme competitiveness, but for some reason they simply wouldn't listen.

In those early days I always got boatmen who knew water, but just didn't have the attitude nor the enthusiasm I wanted on the river. I wanted boatmen who liked people. But in many cases my boatmen made it quite plain that they felt the passengers were just a nuisance.

I had one for instance who was quite religious begin to feel that it was a sin to run the river on Sunday. If he kept it up, he reasoned, he believed God would punish him. I really didn't pay too much attention to this because on the river Sunday is just like any other day. One particular Sunday I arranged for Field and Stream magazine and a number of Eastern

newspaper reporters to fly down from the South Rim of the Grand Canyon to take pictures of my boats negotiating Lava Rapid.

Saturday, Bill had run a rapid called Upset, above Lava and for the first time ever, flipped all three little boats upside down. I, of course, didn't consider this any kind of omen, but he did.

Sunday, the helicopters brought down three loads of top editors and writers from Field and Stream and a number of reporters from large Eastern newspapers. They spent the next couple of hours setting up to take just the right pictures, then we were ready. I shoved off, hit the big hole, buried the big boat in a wall of water, then shot through on the other side. It was a perfect run. Next we were ready for Bill. The cameramen got ready. The tension grew. Suddenly someone ran toward me over the rocks screaming, "Bill won't run the boats. He just turned them loose on the river."

Sure enough, in a minute here they came, three boats riding empty through Lava. As they came abreast of me, one of the men standing beside me ran down to a point on the river and brought the boats into shore.

I just stood there and fumed. Here I had this whole group of Eastern newsmen waiting, and although he knew how important this was to me he deliberately blew it. If he had only mentioned his feeling I could have flown back in the helicopter and run the little boats through myself. As it turned out the reporters simply had to utilize the pictures they had already taken.

This was just one type of problem I

The big boats enabled me to take bigger groups and different types of people—including children and older folks—because we didn't risk upsetting.

had with this group of boatmen. There were others as well. For instance, at my request the National Park Service assigned a ranger, Dan Davis, to go down the river with me and gather information. I have to admit that I was extremely lucky with the choice of this particular ranger. I was already known at the South Rim as that "crazy woman on the river." If they had assigned a ranger who was unhappy be-cause I had gotten him out from behind a desk, I could have been in trouble. All he had to do was go back up there and say, "you're right, that woman is crazy." I was doubly under the gun since the Park Service was already nervous about several deaths which had recently occurred along the river.

As it turned out, it was love at first sight between Dan Davis and the river.

Dan was a professional geologist, and had a keen interest in nature. He was eager to learn all he could about the canyons and the escape routes such as the Hopi trail. These he incorporated with his own observations and knowledge. He also observed my safety precautions and from these, and from other information he had accumulated, he made up the first raft safety rules ever utilized on the Colorado River. He was, in short, a tremendous asset.

Unfortunately I had a boatman on this trip who took an instant dislike to Dan. This particular boatman was extremely intelligent, but looked down on everyone and wanted to be by himself on trips. He thought Dan was entirely too friendly with the passengers and that he did everything wrong.

I didn't think too much about it at the time, but several months after the trip was over I received a letter from the Park Service which simply said that they had received a letter of complaint about Dan Davis and that they would soon hold a hearing. I was stunned. Then I realized that my boatman must have sent that letter. I sat down and wrote a letter praising Dan Davis and listing all the positive things he had done on the trip. As a result he was cleared completely.

At that point it was an understatement to say that I was dissatisfied with the quality of boatmen I was getting. I wanted desperately to find a better solution.

Two fire chiefs from the Los Angeles Fire Department came on the trip. One evening around the campfire I started talking about my boatmen troubles. Finally, one of them said, "Georgie, why don't you try some of our firemen. They are trained to work together as a team and they already have their first-aid training. I think they would make good boatmen for you."

I thought about it that winter and the next year I asked Harry Stiers and Pete Thompson to come along that summer as boatmen. The chiefs, I discovered, were right. These boatmen would listen to what I said, they would cooperate with each other, they had a natural affinity for the river and most important, they were enthusiastic and went out of their way to make sure that everyone else had a good time. They had the exact qualities I needed. For awhile the firemen cut more boats and damaged more motors than the others, but over the years they have just become better and better.

Not all my non-firemen boatmen have been a disappointment. In fact some have been really outstanding and I find it impossible to talk about boatmen, any boatman, without mentioning Orville Miller, a professor from the University of Southern California who knows the Colorado River like the back of his hand. He helped pioneer Mexican river rafting with me, and has been a tremendous help to me on the river for many years.

After saying all those good things about Orville, I now have to admit that the first time I met him on the river he was an absolute disappointment. And if anyone had told me at that time that Orville would eventually become one of my best boatmen, I probably would have told him that he was crazy.

During the days before the Glen Canyon Dam, the Colorado River would start in the early spring with a flow of about 125,000 cubic feet a second and as the summer progressed, the water level would drop to 3000 cubic feet a second and lower. The Glen Canyon Dam had just been authorized by Congress for immediate construction and I knew that when it was finished, the water released from it would stabilize the flow of the Colorado River, year round. This meant that to negotiate the river successfully I would have to run on 8000, 5000 and 3000 cubic feet per second of water and less. I had never run the Colorado River on water this low so I decided I had better take an experimental trip to learn the techniques of low-water running. I wasn't at all sure I could even get through. In fact, I believed that it was quite possible we would become stuck somewhere, have to abandon the raft, and hike out over the cliffs.

I advertised for people to go down the river with me in August, 1956, and to share expenses. I explained this was an experimental trip, that they should be good hikers, and that they should be willing to help with the necessary work. I hoped this appeal would bring good, strong, hard-working people.

I left Lee's Ferry with eight passengers and ran to Phantom Ranch without trouble. Below that I expected rough conditions. Several people left at Phantom, but four more were to hike down the trail from the South Rim to join me. I had great hopes that the new people coming in would provide really good help.

Unfortunately on the way to Phantom I had punctured the middle boat. Under ordinary conditions I could have patched the tiny hole in an hour. But the wind was fierce that day and blew sand everywhere. So I'd patch, and the wind would blow sand, and the patch wouldn't work. I would have to take that patch off and try another. As it turned out I wound up sitting all day trying to patch that hole. Needless to say after the third or fourth patch I was ready to snap at anything. In the meantime the people who had hiked down to join me had passed on the trail while I was busy patching the boat. I finally got the patch to stick and walked the short distance to Phantom where I expected to find my new helpers swimming in the pool. I must say I wasn't prepared for what I saw. There, asleep in one of the chairs, with his mouth wide open and his pack thrown beside the chair, was this long, pale, lean white fellow who looked like he had never done a lick of work in his life.

Was I disappointed. I had counted on getting some real help and this . . . whatever it was . . . had shown up. Disgusted, I just turned around and stalked away without saying a word.

Later I learned that one of the girls couldn't carry her heavy pack so Orville had brought it down the trail for her. This meant he had hiked to the river with nearly one hundred pounds on his back. By the time he reached Phantom Ranch he was exhausted. When I learned that, I was still mad. I needed him to help with the boats not wear himself out helping someone else.

That evening it began to rain and Orville opened a big tarp he had brought with him and asked some of the school teachers from Detroit to sit with him.

They were laughing and drinking wine when I walked up.

Orville motioned to me and asked, "Like a drink?"

I snapped, "I don't need a drink, I can get along without it very well."

Next morning when we pulled out I still had my dander up. For several trips now I had heard rumors that there was a bridge somewhere up a canyon near Mile 140. So I had decided to stop this trip and explore. When I pulled in I took off up that canyon at a furious pace. I kept saying to Orville, "You look tired, why don't you go back?"

Sensing that I was unhappy with him he decided to keep up with me no matter what. All the way up that canyon he stayed right behind me.

When I started back down an hour later, Orville started down too. I turned to him and said, "I've got to rush back to start dinner, don't try to keep up." At that I raced down that hill. When I hit bottom Orville was right beside me. Later he told me that he had almost collapsed, both in going up and coming down, but that he had been determined to show me that he could take it.

The next few days we ran without incident taking the rapids easily. Then on the third day just below Mile 180 we came to Bedrock Rapid. Believe me, it was bad news. I had never seen water that low. On the right a huge sandbar came clear out to the big boulder. Then when I went left the raft hung on the rocks between a rock shelf and the wall.

I studied our predicament for a few minutes then I said to the passengers, "You might as well take pictures before

we get ourselves unstuck. You'll probably never see a sight like this again."

Finally I had them help me take the motor off and let the the air out of the middle boat. Next I asked everyone to climb back in the raft and put all their weight on the portion of the raft that was resting in the swiftest current. Finally I stood in the back and pulled the rear end of the boat up over my head. Slowly we began to ease through and within a few minutes we had pulled free of the rocks. Orville kept very quiet through this whole ordeal but he was watching every move intently.

Later he told me that when he saw that, he had said to himself, "Boy, if she can take a boat through a spot that is six feet too narrow for her boat, then I am going down the river with her forever."

At first Orville went as just another passenger, then he, gradually, became a regular boatman. He would often patch boats, set up, and help with other chores. Gradually we became fast friends and eventually I came to regard him as almost my right-hand man on the river.

Over the years utilizing a combination of firemen and regulars like Orville I have pretty much solved the boatman problem. The ones I take with me now are extremely enthusiastic and have compiled an outstanding safety record on the river. One of the real advantages is that they listen to what I say without resentment. That is not to say that my boatmen do what I tell them at all times. They don't. Once out of my sight I imagine they sometimes cut corners a bit. But it is nothing like it used to be. I'm now called Mama by many of the boatmen and my big boat has become known as Mama's Boat. All in all we've developed a comaraderie that works well.

Boatmen, of course, weren't the only problem I needed to solve once I started handling large groups of people. I also had to become extremely safety conscious. In the early days on the river I often traveled alone out of contact with civilization for up to a month at a time. Under those conditions if I had broken a leg I probably would have died right there. I learned quickly to be extremely careful and to make good safety habits almost automatic.

The three-boats and the big boat that I developed were intrinsically safer than the single ten-man boats. In putting the three-boats together I always kept safety in mind. For instance, I designed a safety line for the three-boat that runs all the way around the outside. If anyone falls in the water he can grab a rope within easy reach. The big boat has two secure handholds per person. I designed the ties so that when you pull on any rope it tightens the other ropes all the way around. The big boat is almost impossible to turn over and if one section gets punctured we have many more sections to keep us afloat.

Carrying food on the river also has a safety aspect besides the obvious one of keeping it in good condition and avoiding food poisoning. In recent years some river outfitters have begun carrying food in large wooden or metal boxes lashed or bolted to a wooden frame. These, in my opinion, are extremely dangerous. Unfortunately several passengers riding on these boxes have been severely injured. In one case a box tore loose in a rapid and broke the legs and backs of the people caught in between. I carry food packed in rubber neoprene

This is Thunder River which drops almost vertically for three-quarters of a mile. The stream gushes from holes high up the canyon to rush to join Tapeats Creek.

bags tied along the sides of the big boat. The passengers here are completely surrounded by rubber. The bags have no sharp angles and a passenger can be thrown against them in a rapid without any danger.

I never want anyone hurt on my trips, so over the years I have laid down stringent safety rules. On my boats I always remind passengers at every rapid to keep their feet up and not catch them between boats. I stress that people hang on and stay with the boat even if they get flipped out in a rapid. I make staying with the boat the cardinal rule because I know that a person will be safer if he stays with the boat in a rapid than if he tried to swim the rapid by himself.

Besides the physical aspects, safety on the river also has its psychological side. People, for instance, watch me intently to make sure I'm back there running the boat. Often in a rapid I'll look up to find a number of passengers staring at me instead of the river. I also get questions: "Do you ever leave the boat, Georgie? If so, how quickly can you get back aboard?" I guess I can understand this, because without me they would be stranded in rough-river country.

I find that people are up tight at any hint of danger. If I so much as check a patch in their sight they become quite upset. I have learned because of this to check my boats early in the morning before anyone gets up. That way everyone stays calm on the river.

I also find that people today are much, much too concerned about the little accidents that occur. On another outfitter's river trip a passenger bruised her finger and asked a boatman to put antiseptic on it. About that time one of the doctor passengers said, "That looks bad; it could become infected." That panicked her and she demanded to be flown out by helicopter. That kind of reaction amazes me. I'm from the old school that just ignores the minor problems.

A couple of seasons ago I cut my finger almost to the bone just before a trip. Instead of rushing to a doctor I bandaged it, threw some peroxide in a bag and left for the river. During the trip I continually exposed the finger to gas, oil and water, but by the time I reached Temple Bar on Lake Mead it had almost healed.

If someone is seriously hurt, of course, I want to take action immediately. But I'm afraid I have little patience with people who become concerned and frightened at every little upset. Fortunately my trips have few major problems and I have the best safety record on the Colorado River. I have never had a fatal accident on any of my boats or even a major one. Over more than thirty years of rapid running however, two people on trips with me have suffered fatal heart attacks, including my very good friend, May, who went with me for years. Fortunately, incidents like this are a rarity.

Besides boatmen and safety, food is a vitally important ingredient on any large river trip. Today I need carry food for only five or six days since on the Grand Canyon trip I pick up additional supplies at Whitmore, a little over halfway down the canyon. There mules bring food down the trail from the canyon rim above. Despite the fact that we can pick up supplemental supplies part way through the trip, forty to eighty people still eat large quantities of food.

I decided early that if I was going to handle these quantities efficiently I would need good organization and standardization. As a result I developed a rather set menu for breakfast, lunch and dinner and a standard way of handling every meal. First, because I don't take ice, I carry only dry or canned foods. Breakfast consists of hot and cold cereal, canned juice and canned fruit. Lunch is cheese, bread and jam, peanut butter, cookies and some kind of meat. For dinner, I rotate about five basic menus: lima beans and ham, spaghetti and green beans and other similar combinations.

To make it easy to handle I package each meal separately in a neoprene bag marked in large letters with the meal and the day it will be served. In the early days everyone did his own cooking. Today my boatmen and I cook on a butane stove. Each passenger brings his own bowl, cup and utensils which he washes individually. I hardboil eggs for a ten-o'clock-in-the-morning egg break, and serve food items such as cereals and bread in a small, blown-up wading pool which I call a "table." The meals are nutritious and my system takes a lot of the work out of handling food. This is important when traveling and serving a lot of people.

The final area I consider important to any trip is the overall atmosphere. This may sound strange but, believe me, it is vital. People today come on the river to relax and to enjoy themselves. Over the years I've discovered that the best way to help them do this is to provide a jovial, friendly, kidding atmosphere.

I promote this with my own attitude. The boatmen and passengers add to my efforts with their own personalities. For instance I discourage small cliques and try to promote my group as one big family. I always tell people that they are never alone on a river trip. A person may be a lone man or a lone woman or a grand-parent, but on the river we're all just companions. In the early years I wouldn't let anyone discuss their occupations. I wanted the doctors and the lawyers and the secretaries and the plumbers to all be on the same footing. I don't enforce this today. But often you'll find a famous surgeon with six days' growth of beard, dressed in cutoffs, helping to push a boat off a sandbar shoulder to shoulder with a truck driver from Chicago.

I realized that people who run rivers like to feel they have done something special, so I decided several years ago to give river runners a symbol to commemo-rate the trip.

One day I happened to glance over at a group who had just come through a rapid. They looked awful. They were soaked to the skin, their clothes clung to their bodies and their hair stuck to their faces. They looked, I decided, like rats. At that time I coined the name, "river rats." But I decided that since the Colorado River has the biggest rapids in the United States, if you ran the Grand Canyon, you weren't just a river rat, you were a "Royal River Rat."

At that time I had a passenger taking the trip to take pictures for a winter lec-ture tour. He didn't like the name river rats. Soon he began calling us "canyon-eers." Somehow that didn't sound like water and he got a terrible response. After that he changed the name back to river rats and it went over big.

From then on river rats stuck. People loved it and new people on the river always looked forward to becoming river rats. Over the years I have also utilized the name to stand for my commercial river operation. I get special joy from seeing the look on a motel clerk's face when he asks who I represent and I say, "Georgie's Royal River Rats."

I have to admit that I generally en-courage horseplay on the river. I think it helps develop a camaraderie. For instance, anyone who falls asleep on the big boat gets doused with a bucket of water from almost everybody. Sometimes the boatmen will grab everybody who comes along (including me) and give them a head to foot mud bath along the river banks.

More river life: the water-dousing initiation that turns you into a river rat; an injured outboard; and the roughest patch of water between Lee's Ferry and Lake Mead.

Frequently fifteen to twenty people will wind up struggling in that slippery mud. Afterwards they clean up by dunking themselves in the river. Antics like these add to all river trips and I generally encourage boatmen to engage in them. Some of my boatmen such as Orville Miller, don't need much encouragement, they just come to it naturally.

On the USC campus I'm sure Orville is quite dignified, but on the river he is a combination devil, tease, little boy, wise man, and father figure. He is just exactly what I need! Being a chemist, Orville makes his own Mexican cactus sun tan oil. And at the drop of a hat he will give anyone a massage. He has also concocted a horrible purple medicine he carries for cuts and bruises. By the end of his trips practically everyone walks around with these ugly looking purple blotches all over their arms and legs. Whenever I see them I say to myself, "Orville has struck again."

Of course Orville always has some

practical joke up his sleeve so you must be on guard if you don't want to wind up a victim. For instance, one afternoon while I was bending over working on a raft, Orville walked up behind me and took a picture without my knowledge. That winter he had the picture enlarged, bought an old toilet seat and pasted a picture of my rear end over the seat. At the end of the next trip I received this toilet seat and my picture signed by all the boatmen. Next, Orville blew up a picture of my face, put a huge nude body on it and presented that to me at the end of the trip.

Actually these are his milder practical jokes; some become pretty physical. In one case, Orville and another boatman, Ray Olson, carried me bodily into the water, unfastening the top of my bathing suit as we went off the bank. When I came out a few minutes later there was Orville shouting, "Georgie's gone topless. Georgie's gone topless." He, of course, had alerted everyone so they would be on hand to take pictures.

Sometimes these tricks backfire. In the early days Orville and other boatmen used to sneak up at night while I was sleeping, untie my boat and shove it out in the river. When this happened I just let the boat drift across the river and didn't come back until after breakfast. That meant whoever turned me loose had to fix breakfast for the whole camp. A time or two of this and they decided not to pull that trick anymore.

Now and then, I managed to strike back at Orville. After one trip in which he teased the women unmercifully I took them aside and said, "When we reach Temple Bar I want all of you to wrestle him to the ground and take away his

pants." When we pulled in, the girls asked him to come to the lake with them.

Of course he went. When they reached the shore everyone grabbed him, wrestled him to the ground, took away his pants and left him running around in his shorts. Orville is a big fellow, but he just didn't have a chance with all those girls. A couple of minutes later I heard a bellow, "This was Georgie's idea!" I jumped up, rushed to the restroom a quarter of a mile away, locked myself in, and didn't come out until I knew Orville had gone on to the restaurant.

Boatmen, of course, don't have a monopoly on river fun, and often passengers like to get in on the act. One of the people who always came up with elaborate jokes was Marshall Bond, Jr., of Santa Barbara. Marshall looked exactly like the serious businessman he was, but he always did such outlandish things that he just broke people up. For instance, on one of my Glen Canyon trips Marshall decided to act as official greeter. When the other passengers arrived the next day, Marshall, dressed in a top hat, tux jacket, and bathing suit bottom, was strutting up and down the beach greeting everyone. Another time he showed up with a razor about the size of a thimble. I always enjoy having people like Marshall on my trips since they help break the ice and create a relaxed, friendly atmosphere.

Once horseplay is encouraged, then everyone wants to get in on the act. At one of the campsites one evening, I had to stand ankle deep in water to cook supper. I had mentioned I wanted to change shoes, so when a doctor, who had gone with me many times, told me to go ahead and he would turn off dinner, I didn't think anything about it. When I came back and noticed all the cameras I still didn't catch on. Then I opened the pot I had been heating, and there on top of the meat balls was a cow's skull with gravy coming out its eyes. Was I startled! This kind of fun always brings people together. At the end of that trip, everyone was like one big friendly family.

Not everything we do on the river, of course, involves horseplay. Over the years we've made some serious discoveries, often quite by accident. One morning in the mid-fifties, we were on our way downriver near Unkar, when one of the passengers asked me to pull over for a bathroom stop. Since he didn't have any cover on the river bank he hiked over a small hill and disappeared from sight. A few minutes later he ran back screaming, "Georgie, there's every kind of pottery up there!"

Sure enough, he had made a major find. There were literally hundreds of perfect pieces in every imaginable color. After that we stopped every trip to take pictures.

A few years later several universities catalogued everything there and removed all the pottery. It was, I am told, one of the largest finds on the river, and will in the future add a great deal to our knowledge of these Indians and their skills.

*   *   *

One winter I received a letter from a man who said his ambition was to run the Colorado River. Somewhere in the letter he mentioned that his age was eighty-six. I just shook my head. I wanted to encourage older people to try the river experience, but eighty-six?

A few days later I received another letter. "Don't pay any attention to that old fool," it said. "He isn't in his right mind."

That did it. I wrote back and said I couldn't take him. Four days later I answered a knock on the door and there stood my eighty-six-year-old prospective river rat.

"I really want to go," he told me. "I'm in good physical health. I'll do anything you say."

"And that second letter?"

"That's from my wife; she doesn't want me to do anything."

"Okay," I told him, "no hiking, and you must handle your own baggage and not get in the way."

He agreed. On the trip he was perfect. He helped with the meals frequently and each morning he carried his baggage to the boat long before I was ready to leave. When we reached Lake Mead, the Boulder City, Nevada newspaper had gotten wind that we had just come through the canyon with the oldest person to ever run the river so they sent a reporter to Temple Bar to interview him.

"It was the greatest experience of my life," he told the reporter.

"Are you going again?"

"I'll be going until I am 92," he said, "if Georgie can hold up that long." It's incidents like these that make the river enjoyable for me.

When talking about river trips and the people who make them, of course, I can't forget Sambo. Sambo wasn't a person but a large black dog who went down the river with me for many years. I first met Sambo when my sister Marie opened our back gate one night and a dog walked in. He had a license so I called his owner. "We gave him to friends," the owner told me. "Since they don't seem to care for him you can have the dog."

"Put it in writing," I told her. "I don't want to fall in love with him and then have to give him back."

She did, and Sambo became a permanent fixture on my trips. He had his own orange life jacket, a comb, bowl, and sleeping bag. Whenever I was ready to head downriver, Sambo would jump up by the motor mount and I would snap on his leash. When we came to rapids I would reach over and tie him in so he couldn't fall overboard. When we landed Sambo would jump up and down until I turned him loose. He couldn't stand to have anyone beat him ashore. Most of the time Sambo was great but once in awhile he did become a bit of a nuisance.

On my trip down the Big Bend of the Columbia River at Golden, British Columbia, the mosquitoes that first evening had become a terrible bother. I got tired of brushing hundreds of them off my arms, legs and face and had crawled into my sleeping bag early.

Sometime during the night Sambo left his sleeping bag on the boat and headed ashore. The mosquitoes came after him in droves. At first he didn't pay any attention, then he couldn't take it any longer and jumped in the river. Finally he came running back and dove head first into my sleeping bag. I sat bolt upright. My whole bag was absolutely soaked. I started to

crawl out but the mosquitoes buzzed threateningly. I sighed, remembering the hoards of mosquitoes that had covered my arms and face earlier and decided that it was better to stay here with Sambo than to expose myself again. Needless to say I wasn't very happy, but Sambo seemed quite satisfied and quickly settled down to sleep out the rest of the night in comfort.

One of our traditions on the river is blackberry liqueur in coffee or cocoa. I used to take a couple of bottles along in the early days. Then a Swedish passenger said, "Georgie have you tried this in coffee?" A tradition was born. After that I began to take more and more on the trip. Now almost everybody indulges in blackberry and coffee before the evening meal.

At the end of every trip we also have a river rat initiation to keep the tradition going and for the fun of it. The initiates crawl around on the ground blindfolded and throw water at each other. Surprisingly no one ever seems to feel these initiations are too childish. I made the mistake one time of not including a paper company executive because he seemed so dignified. He was so disappointed that later, on another trip, he and I rigged a joke where I appeared to push him off a high cliff into the Colorado River. That seemed to make up for everything.

I generally like to take all sorts of people on the river, but in the early days of running I began a policy of not taking celebrities. I have nothing against celebrities but I want my trips run a certain way and to have a definite atmosphere. Unfortunately, celebrities have a habit of taking over and projecting their own personalities on a trip. If they don't, then generally the manager or someone else connected with their party tries to do it.

A good example of this is the Bureau of Reclamation trip with Bobby Kennedy of 1966. This started out as a very straightforward trip; unfortunately, the people with Kennedy took over and turned it into a three-ring circus.

Generally, enough food is carried on rafts for at least half the trip. Naturally, it's necessary to compromise. As I mentioned, I carry only canned food, but on other boats, by utilizing large wooden boxes, they manage to serve steak every night.

The Kennedy aides decided that even this wasn't nearly good enough. So every day, a helicopter flew back and forth between the river and the South Rim to bring in gourmet food. This is not my idea of roughing it in the wilderness. I wouldn't allow it on my trips and actually, if I had my way, would ban helicopters from the canyon completely.

The helicopter episode was just the beginning. At Nankoweap Canyon, the Indians built a number of structures several hundred feet up on the canyon wall. Until a few years ago, I stopped here every trip and have taken people from eight to seventy years old up to Nankoweap. When Bobby Kennedy climbed Nankoweap, the headlines suddenly screamed, "Kennedy Stuck in Ruins." Let me tell you from personal experience, no one gets stuck at Nankoweap. The openings are just too large. I believe one of his aides dreamed the idea up as a publicity ploy. After all, he was running for election and this was a good way to get attention.

I supported Kennedy and his politics, but I don't appreciate the Grand Canyon being misused in this way, and I absolutely don't want anything like this happening on any of my trips.

The fact that celebrities and important people tend to take over was brought home forcefully several years ago when a very prominent California judge decided that I was going to change the dates of my Mexican trip to suit his schedule. I didn't, but he put me under a lot of pressure before he finally gave up.

After that, my celebrity experience became almost comical. One of these unusual episodes occurred with the Barry Goldwater staff from Tucson, Arizona.

First, the people from the Goldwater office applied to me as a group. My sister, Marie, took one look at the application, then wrote back and said we just couldn't take them that year. I thought that would be the end of it.

Next year, the reservations began to come in early for the following summer. Marie came to me one night and said, "I'm not sure, Georgie, since I haven't kept track, but I think a lot of those people from the Goldwater staff have sent in reservations again. This time, they're sending in names separately."

When we looked, sure enough, there they were.

"Should I cancel?" she asked.

"No," I said. "If they want to go that badly, I'll take them."

When they showed up, I told them, "My trips are one big happy family, so I'd appreciate it if you would mix with everyone on the trip." They did exactly that and we had a tremendous time.

On another trip, a rather undistinguished, middle-aged man with a beard and tattered jeans showed up, driving a dilapidated old car. I didn't pay much attention, but halfway through the trip, one of the passengers came to me and said, "Georgie, that man is a senator. I've seen his pictures a million times."

I didn't say anything right away. Then one night I asked him about it.

"Yes, Georgie, I'm a senator, but please let me be as inconspicuous as possible. I'm here to just get away and relax."

I said that was fine with me, and through the rest of the trip he remained just one of the passengers.

Those were really exciting, adventurous years on the Colorado River. Without a doubt, I was beginning to achieve my goal of opening river experience to everyone. Throughout the many years I have been running rivers, my sister, Marie, has always been my backup. She has taken river reservations, kept the books, run errands, bought supplies, and performed a thousand other chores no one else could do. While I've always been on the river where people could see me, Marie has done an equal share behind the scenes. I've always said that I couldn't do without her, and I mean it.

About this time, several things were happening. First, the Bureau of Reclamation completed Glen Canyon Dam and filled Lake Powell, burying Glen Canyon forever. Now, instead of the giant 125,000 cubic feet runoff that I had been used to in the spring, the water release year round,

varied between 4000 and 8000 cubic feet per second. The driftwood, which constantly plagued us in the big water days, now dropped to almost nothing since most of it was trapped behind the dam.

Up until the dam was constructed, I had been one of the very few trying to take large groups down the Colorado River. But then, when the dam was finished, the Park Service assigned commercial concessions. Suddenly, over a dozen operators appeared to take people down the river. And simultaneously, almost overnight, river running became extremely popular all over the United States. Believe me, it was quite a feeling. A few years before, when I mentioned wild rivers, everyone looked at me like I was crazy. Now, I had become a hero to certain groups of people, as river running became a very popular outdoor sport.

With all this activity, of course, things began to change. The more people who came on the river, the more the Park Service and other agencies began to regulate the sport. These regulations were few at first, then they began to affect the number of people who could go down the river in a single season, whether or not you could build open fires, the drinking water, the type of training you gave the boatmen, and more. At first I wasn't sure how I felt about all this. It seemed that once my goal was in sight, it was suddenly being taken away. But I realize that that is how things are in life.

The days of river pioneering in North America are really over. It was the last frontier to be conquered.

Rivers of the North

I guess you might say I receive the same satisfaction running rivers that an artist gets from expressing his feelings on canvas, or that a pole vaulter feels making a high jump without disturbing the bar. I shall never tire of this feeling, and no matter how many times I've run the Colorado River, the challenge of reading the currents and running the rapid just right will always excite me.

Despite the fact that I derive a great deal of pleasure from the Colorado River, I'm still an extremely restless person who thrives on action and adventure. As a result, it was only natural that at the time I was trying to master the rapids of the Colorado, I would also look for other rivers to challenge.

During the early years of river exploration, I carried a small raft in my truck and whenever I found interesting water, I'd unload the raft and go for a run. This is the way I tried Rogue River, Oregon, the Virgin River, Utah, and others.

One time when a storm hit Los Angeles, the dry, cement-lined rivers there became swollen torrents of water. Los Angeles generally receives very little rainfall each year, so most of the time these rivers are bone dry. The city and county of Los Angeles paved the stream bed along many of them and in some cases, have temporarily allowed golf courses to occupy them. When the skies open up and pour, as they sometimes do in Southern California, then it is a different story. Water rushes off the hills and turns those streambeds into angry, boiling monsters.

During one storm, I launched my raft in somebody's backyard and went whirling along just below the houses, traffic and stores. It was a fast ride. Then I rounded a bend and crashed smack into a barbed wire fence stretched across the river. Because of the force of the current it took me a couple of minutes to untangle the raft and push it to shore. When I finally crawled out, blood was running down my arms and legs from the long scratches I received from the barbed wire. My wounds were superficial and I knew I'd heal quickly, so I simply took a bus back to my truck, picked up my raft and headed home.

I had heard a great deal about the Salmon River in Idaho, the famous "River of No Return." The Big Salmon and the middle fork of the Salmon River run most of the way across the state of Idaho through the Sawtooth Primitive Area. Magazine and television reports would have you believe that the Salmon was one of the roughest, wildest rivers in the country. In addition, people I talked to kept telling me about the huge rapids on the Salmon River. I was always looking for good, white water adventure, and so naturally, with this build-up of the Big Salmon and the middle fork of the Salmon, I was really intrigued. By 1954 my curiosity got the best of me, so I decided that year I would run the Salmon River for the first time.

The second week of August, 1954, I drove to McCall, Idaho, with nine ten-man rubber life rafts and enough supplies for an eighteen-day trip. Here I met twenty-seven men and women of all ages from all over the United States who wanted to take the trip with me. We drove to the airport where I had hired the Johnson Flying Service of McCall to fly us up the middle fork of the Salmon where we would launch the nine rafts.

I was taken aback. I had, of course, flown in dozens of small planes, but the tri-motor Ford aircraft waiting there on the runway was a real antique. I thought they had been phased out of service long before this. I discovered that the Forest Service used these planes quite extensively to train and fly smoke jumpers.

Thirty-five minutes later, the pilots put us down at Indian Landing on the middle fork of the Salmon River, "The River of No Return." From here, I would run eighty miles of the middle fork, then join the Big Salmon for the additional one hundred and twenty miles to my take-out point at Riggin's Hot Springs.

On that first trip down the Salmon, I met Barry Goldwater who was there on a rafting and fishing trip. The river was low and rocky that year and the Goldwater party was running just in front of me. When they pulled into the lodge down-river, their guide figured that since I was new on the Salmon, I would probably get hung up on the rocks and not show for hours. Barry Goldwater knew of my reputation on the Colorado River, however, so he just laughed.

"I'm surprised," he said, "that she didn't beat us in."

As it turned out, I pulled up about ten minutes later. I knew the senator had run the Colorado River several times with Nevills, so we spent the next half hour talking about this.

From the minute I launched those rafts, the trip became an eye-opener, and a tremendous disappointment. I expected real wilderness there but I never found it. On the Colorado River then, I could run eight to nine hundred miles without seeing any signs of civilization. But all the way down the Salmon, we kept passing dozens of lodges where you could stop and buy film, beer, ice cream, and all the other refinements I had hoped to leave behind.

I admit that most of the lodges were only accessible by plane, but we certainly weren't running through a wilderness. This was my first disappointment. The second one came when we reached the rapids. The biggest rapid on the middle fork was Grouse Creek. When we ran it, we came downriver, hit the tongue, bounced across a couple of waves, dropped about four feet down a rocky chute, then shot out into calm water again.

This rapid didn't begin to compare with even the medium-sized rapids on the Colorado River. But I told myself that this was only the rocky middle fork. Maybe when we joined the Big Salmon in a few miles, we would find the really big rapids I'd heard so much about. That, too, proved a disappointment. During that 120-mile run to Riggin's Hot Springs, we did go over several sharp drops and ran through some fairly long rocky runs, but I found nothing that I would really call a rapid.

In my opinion, even in those days, the Salmon River was not much of a white water trip. Unfortunately in later years, they blasted away the biggest rapid on the

Big Salmon to bring the jet boats upstream. I could never really understand why they destroyed their best rapid, but then I guess the residents decided it was more important to get boats upstream fast to their lodges than to keep a rapid just for pleasure. At the end of the trip I concluded that the middle fork and the Big Salmon are just not good rivers for people who enjoy the excitement of running big rapids.

The green-timbered Idaho mountains along the way are, of course, beautiful, the hunting and fishing excellent, and the residents friendly, so it makes a good combination trip for people who enjoy those activities.

I, however, have always felt so strongly about preserving animal life that I have never hunted nor fished nor have I allowed hunting or fishing on any of my trips. As a result I didn't feel the Salmon offered nearly as good a white water trip for me as the Colorado River. Despite this, a number of people who went with me on the Salmon kept asking that I run it again. So I continued to schedule this trip once a year for the next four years. Not surprisingly, the most memorable events that occurred on those trips had nothing to do with rapids.

The first memorable experience took place on my second trip in 1954. We were on our way down the middle fork about fifty miles above the confluence with the Big Salmon. A passenger about seventy years old was sitting in the back of my boat taking pictures of the passing scenery. Suddenly he took two short breaths, gasped, and keeled over in the boat. A doctor in the front of the boat jumped up and rushed back. It was too late. He had suffered a heart attack in the middle of picture taking, and died.

I said to the doctor, "People panic so easily that I'd rather not tell anyone that he's dead. Let's cover him up and send him out at the nearest landing strip." When we reached a lodge a few miles downstream, the other boats had already pulled in. I simply told them that he had become sick and had to leave.

The only other person who knew about the death was a friend of the dead man who made arrangements to fly him to Salmon, Idaho, by plane, and then ship his body home. I have thought about this incident a number of times since, and I feel this is probably a good way to die. I sincerely hope that when my time comes that I too will leave right in the middle of an activity I enjoy.

The next incident that stands out in my memory occurred two years later. It had nothing to do with rapids or death, but concerns the State of Idaho and the politics of river running. Because the Sierra Club had run big rafts down the Salmon River several years before, the Salmon River outfitters (commercial river guides) had convinced the state to pass a license requirement for river runners. This way, those outfitters who lived in Idaho and ran the river on a regular basis would have an advantage over someone from out of state who ran only once a year. I decided before I left home that I didn't believe in licensing river adventurers and that I wouldn't buy a license. I also decided that if I were forced into it I would pay a fine, but they had to catch me first.

Apparently someone turned me in, because the authorities knew I was on the river my second day out. There is a shallow rocky spot on the river near one of the resorts where many of the boats get stuck. Here, three state game wardens waded out in the water on a rocky point and waited for me to run aground so they could give me a notice of violation.

The minute I came around the bend and saw the three men standing there, I knew what they wanted. I blew my top. No way were they going to hand me a violation notice without a fight. I simply bounced across that shallow spot and rode on through into deeper water, while the wardens watched helplessly. I have to admit it tickled me to see them standing out there on the rocks, unable to reach my boat. After I returned to Los Angeles, I realized that the state would probably try to make trouble, so I sent the money. But I still absolutely detest the idea of a state licensing rafting and I have never gone back since to run either the middle fork or the Big Salmon itself.

There was also one other thing that bothered me about the Salmon River in those days, and that was that the residents sometimes let their sewage empty directly into the side streams. I always told my "river rats" to take their drinking water directly out of the main river since the water in a fast stream purifies itself in a short distance. But I had one passenger who absolutely insisted on drinking from the side streams. Finally, I stopped at one of the lodges I knew about and asked the owner, a woman, if we could use her bathroom facilities.

"Help yourself," she said, and pointed down a trail to an outhouse. I took the whole group to the outhouse which sat out over a small stream that led directly to the main river.

"Just remember, next time you want to drink out of the side streams, that this isn't the only outhouse you'll find along this particular river," I said. I didn't have any trouble after that.

Whenever I ran the Salmon River, I always took the rafts out of the Big Salmon at Riggin's Hot Springs and trucked them over to Homestead, Oregon, where I ran the Snake River as a continuation of the trip.

Sometimes, on the Snake, I would be joined by Bill Stubblefield, a resident of the area who had been running the river successfully for a number of years. Bill was a big greying man who always gave me a friendly welcome whenever I met him on the river. On the 1955 trip, he decided to take his boat through the first rapid, Kinney Creek, with us to see how our three lashed rafts would ride together. This three-raft concept was a new one on the Snake and people who weren't familiar with how well these boats took the rapids were always curious. I can understand this, because on the water, they look like a pretty awkward combination.

When we came to Kinney Creek Rapid, the water tossed our rafts back and forth as if they were riding a roller coaster, then dropped us gently into the water below. That was an easy rapid.

Not long after that, we encountered a long, rock-studded catarac called Squaw Creek. This proved to be a bit hair-raising. A giant fang of water loomed over us as we came in. The leading raft tilted crazily, and the boats pitched and turned, then shot us out into smooth water. That was the sec-

ond most difficult rapid on the river. Finally about a mile further downstream, we hit Buck Creek Rapid, the roughest one of them all on the Snake River. This rapid had upset a lot of boats in the past and had acquired quite a reputation. This trip, the rafts plunged suddenly over a precipice and completely submerged us in the roaring water. Wham! The boats slammed against a solid wall of water, the front raft stood almost on end, then discharged us out the other side.

From this point to the end of the trip, at Lewiston, Idaho, we ran four more rapids, several riffles and a number of miles of smooth water. The scenery along the Snake was fabulous, with green pines, mountains and rocky cliffs reflected in the water.

I always considered this 154 miles of the Snake River exciting and well worth the effort. Unfortunately, after the power company completed the third dam on this river about 1967, the backwater all but destroyed the rapids. After that, I quit taking trips in this area. I understand, of course, that dams are needed for both power and water, but politics played a great role in the final dam placement. Wild white water has a very low political priority, but, I think that it would have been worth the trouble to have made a greater effort to save the only really good rapids in the Pacific Northwest.

In addition to running the Salmon and Snake rivers, I also became interested in exploring rivers in Alaska. Again, I had heard that some of these rivers contained tremendous rapids and I was anxious to see for myself just what kind of white water lay to the north. The question was which rivers to explore, and how to get there. I needed some very detailed answers to these questions.

My photographer friend, Joe Muench, had started to take a number of trips to both Alaska and Canada, conducting Thru-the-Lens Tours. These tours generally are led by an expert photographer and go all over the world to teach tour members how to photograph what they see. When he came back from the tours, he said, "Georgie, the only river I think you will like is the Copper River near Cordova, Alaska."

The Copper River and its tributary, the Chitina, I discovered are fierce wild rivers rising out of some of the most spectacular mountainous country in the world. The mountains are known as the Alps of Alaska. The peaks in this area are quite jagged, rising to well over 12,000 feet with shiny white glaciers of ice flowing down many of the valleys. Below the snowy crowns is an undulating green blanket of thick, almost impassable forest, populated with numerous animals including bear, moose, sheep, and goats. I decided to check out the Copper River by mail from Los Angeles. What a job that was! I wrote to the Cordova Airline and several other sources asking how to get into the Copper River. They wrote back asking why I wanted to know. Nobody was running rivers in Alaska at that time, and they just couldn't seem to understand why I would want to take a large raft on the Copper River.

I must have written fifty letters before I worked out all the details. After I made the arrangements, I asked the eleven river rats going with me to meet at the Windsor

We loaded the rafts, supplies and ourselves into the DC3 in Cordova, Alaska, to be flown to McCarthy where we started down the Chitina and Copper Rivers.

Hotel in Cordova the last week of August. Flying from Seattle, I arrived in Cordova in the middle of a driving downpour. Ohmer Waer, the owner of the Windsor Hotel, met me at the airport and drove me into town.

This part of Alaska receives 250 inches of rainfall a year and I soon learned that on these trips you can expect part of that rain to fall almost every day. Some days, the rain came down in driving torrents, creating miserable running conditions. Other days the clouds hung low over the peaks and valleys, and still other times, the sun would play hide-and-seek behind dark clouds that occasionally opened up and poured.

The Copper River trip was plagued by rain and big pieces of ice that broke off the glaciers —making us really appreciate the campfire and hot coffee.

I can easily tolerate rain. After all, I have run in some tremendous downpours during the Mexican rainy season. But there is something about those dull gray days and ever-present rain clouds that bothers me. I won't say it depresses me, but I must admit I am a sun person, and I'm always happy to get back to the Arizona-Nevada desert where I can expect to find sunshine at least 300 days a year.

The next day, I loaded the rafts, supplies and the twelve of us on a DC-3 and flew to Mays Creek landing at McCarthy, Alaska. The town itself had been abandoned by the Kennicott Mining Company in 1942. McCarthy looked like one of those quaint old mining towns right out of the gold rush days. To top this off, the town was cradled by at least a dozen high, snow-capped peaks and the Kennicott Glacier. The glacier came almost down to the main street where the twenty-four big tanks used to process copper were slowly being encased in ice.

As we walked around town, we discovered merchandise still on display in the hardware store windows; the dentist drills in the dentist office were still laid out as if the dentist had just stepped out for coffee. The poker hands were still on the tables in the saloon as if the players would be right back. What an eerie feeling! It reminded me of the movie, "On The Beach."

Inside the Golden Hotel Saloon and pool hall, we decided to relive history. One rather short, husky woman wearing floppy shoes and cover-alls, got up and danced while we played the victrola and pounded out the beat on a tub. Laughing hysterically, the whole group joined the dance.

Several of the men picked up the poker hands and played them out. Another took on the role of bartender and made us drink from the almost full bottles left behind the bar.

When we got ready to go to bed, we simply threw our sleeping bags out on the cots in the long dormitory and hung large pieces of burlap between them for privacy. It was an experience I never had before and haven't had since. We didn't have time to explore the mine, but we were told that it contained over eighty-five miles of tunnel.

Next day, we flew from Mays Creek landing to Jake's Bar on the Chitina River. The plane sent to fly us was so small that they had to fly several trips to get the equipment and river rats to the departure point. I'll never forget that first trip. The engine roared and the plane picked up speed, shot down the rocky field that served as a runway, and then dropped sharply into the canyon. Because of the weight, it had yet to reach flying speed. When they asked if I wanted to go with the next load of rafts, I mentally added my weight plus that of the rafts and politely declined.

On the other end of Jake's Bar, the plane circled, dropped into the narrow canyon, leveled out just above water, and set down on a short rocky stretch beside the river. I couldn't believe they could put that plane into such an impossible spot. But the pilot repeated that performance six more times that morning. I gained a lot of respect for those Alaskan bush pilots on that trip. Since that time, I have learned that this is considered standard procedure, and frequently they are called upon to perform much more difficult feats than this.

Next morning, we broke camp at

seven-thirty, and shoved the raft off into the swift angry current of the Chitina River. Native Alaskans, in the wilderness, have what I consider to be an unreasonable paranoic fear of bears. Everywhere I went, I heard horror stories about bears tearing people to bits. Practically everyone I met in Alaska felt it was necessary to carry guns when in the brush. Of course, I have never carried a gun myself. Because I don't believe in guns and don't want animals harmed in any way, I won't let anyone else carry a gun on my trips. Before we left to go on this trip, I had quite an argument with an Alaskan who wanted to run the Copper River with me. Finally, with great apprehension, he left his rifle at home.

About ten that first morning, one of the women with us decided she needed a bathroom stop. The rest of the group groaned. No one wanted to pull in at this point. I, however, pulled the rafts over to the bank where she crawled out and disappeared behind some bushes. Suddenly she started screaming, "Bear . . . bear," and burst into view holding up her pants with one hand. Behind her, a grizzly bear stood on his hind legs watching the whole scene. This was really the only close call, if it can be called that, that we had in Alaska. I know that many people there feel I am foolish for traveling without firearms, but I always take precautions like never leaving food lying around, getting rid of all garbage, and avoiding cooking foods like bacon that give off strong odors. As a result, I never seem to have any real trouble.

At the junction of the Copper and Chitina Rivers, we pulled in on a sandbar and hiked to the small town of Chitina. At the lodge we met Susan, a sixty-three-year-old Athabascan Indian woman. Every time we spoke to Susan, she would break into a tribal dance of welcome. I had, by this time, been around Navajos a great deal, so I enjoyed comparing Susan's life in Alaska with that of the desert Indians. That day, Susan was very tired, since she had been up all night protecting her fish cache from a bear. This was to be her winter supply of smoked fish and she didn't want to lose any of it. Next morning, we hiked back to the river in the ever-present rain and headed downstream.

Before we began this trip, I had heard rumors about some tremendous rapids that existed on the Copper River. The rumors were that at certain times of the year, these rapids were all but impossible to run in rubber rafts. Here was that old rapid-exaggeration hoax popping up again. Somehow, all rivers get built up out of all proportion.

We did find one rapid, Abercrombie Rapid, that did give us a challenge. We had been watching for it several days after joining the Copper, then suddenly one morning, we swept around a bend and there it was. A huge wave suddenly lifted us up, then we shot over the brink and down into an enormous gaping hole. The shock of the collision seemed to stop the rafts completely for a minute then the motor alternately churned and roared as it dipped through three more huge waves. As quickly as it had began, the rapid ended, and we were running in fast smooth water once again. During the rest of the trip, we encountered a few ripples, but nothing to compare with Abercrombie Rapid.

The rain plagued us during the whole trip. Sometimes we made camp or traveled

At the end of the Copper River trip we were greeted by this sign. These local residents have great respect for the swift and icy currents that swirl through their river.

in heavy rain; other times we could see part way up the glacier-filled canyons where swirling clouds cut off the top of the peaks. Big pieces of ice kept breaking off from the glaciers along the way and floated by us in the water.

The current itself was absolutely treacherous. One time, I pulled up on a sandbar, when suddenly the current caught the motor and turned it under the boat. The banks here dropped off so steeply that although one end of the boat was resting on a sandbar, the motor was still out in the swift current. The force is so strong that if you don't get the motor up, the current will double it under almost immediately.

On practically every riffle, ice-cold water poured into the boats, sending shiv-

ers down my spine. It came right off the glaciers and had ice floating in it and was the coldest water I had ever run in. The local people fear this current which is heavily silted with glacial milk, and claim that you can't live more than seven minutes in the icy water. Fortunately, none of us was tossed into the water this trip. I do know that while I enjoyed the ride and the scenery, I didn't particularly want to go swimming in the Copper River.

Six days after leaving McCarthy, we swept under the bridge fifty miles from Cordova, marking the end of our trip. A Volkswagen bus from the Windsor Hotel waited for us on the road and a big sign taped across one side said, "Welcome Glacier Rats."

Then, I began hearing the chop-chop of

a motor. A couple of minutes later, a helicopter came over the ridge and sat down on the road a few hundred feet away. A number of prominant Cordovan people stepped out. They had brought refreshments to help celebrate our successful trip.

As a trip, this one on the Copper River had a lot of advantages. Our experience in the town of McCarthy was probably worth the entire trip to Alaska and the scenery was the most spectacular I've ever seen. As for the rapids, I've been running the Colorado for so long that I always measure rapids on other rivers against the ones I've encountered there. Rated on this scale, the Copper just doesn't stack up. Taking everything into consideration, however, the trip was well worth the effort.

Several years later, an official from Cordova Airlines flew down to California and asked me to run the Copper River on a regular basis. They had, by this time, begun a commercial river operation there, but apparently, it had not been too successful. I considered it for awhile, but then said no. I must admit that if I had considered running any North Country river on an exclusive basis, the Copper would have been that river. However, as I mentioned before, I don't think I could survive the Alaskan rain. I really think it takes a special type of personality to live there year-round.

On that first trip, after a short layover in Cordova, we flew on to Seward on the Kenai Peninsula where I hired a truck to take the boats and passengers out to Kenai Lake. From here I intended to run down the Kenai River about sixty miles to the coast. The trip was short, but it gave us a chance to see another type of Alaskan scenery. The Kenai River, I soon learned, had its own hazards. Here the river ran through what almost looked like tidal country, and the timber on each side of the stream lay back at least two miles from the water. I pulled in for lunch and set the stove up about fifty feet from the water to heat coffee water. Anywhere else in the world this would have been far enough back from the water to avoid any trouble. I turned around a few minutes to talk to someone and when I turned, the water was lapping at the stove and still rising. I gasped, grabbed it on the run and dashed up the bank. Before I reached the top, the rising tide had already covered the spot where I had just been heating coffee. Unknown to me, this coast has probably the second highest tide in the world. And when it starts to rise, it comes fast. I considered myself lucky to have saved that stove.

As we proceeded downriver, I kept noticing what looked like bear tracks. That puzzled me. Here on the tidal flat the timber was at least a mile and a half away from the river, and generally bears avoid open country like this. Sometime later, I discovered that at high tide, hundreds of salmon swim in here then become stranded on the beach when the tide goes out. The bears simply walk out at low tide and pick up their dinner.

Now we were nearing the ocean. The river had become at least half a mile wide. I knew the town of Kenai was nearby, but I couldn't see it. Perhaps it was out of sight up one of the inlets that branched off the main river. I had to make a decision soon. Suddenly someone shouted, "Boat." Straight ahead drifted two men in a rowboat. They had lost their oars a couple of hours earlier and were now floating helplessly on the tide. We stopped and took them in tow.

"You're lucky you found us," one of them told me. "Right now, you are heading out to sea. You're also lucky we have a high tide, otherwise you'd have to beach these rafts miles from the nearest road."

Once again, luck was with me. Soon we landed and sent the rafts by truck on to the airstrip. There we saw the planes were landing on a steel mesh to keep their tires from sinking out of sight in the mud of the unpaved runways.

From here I was supposed to fly directly to Guatemala to begin another trip in a few days. Unfortunately, however, the Alaskan weather simply didn't cooperate and for several days the chartered plane that I hired simply couldn't land. The swirling clouds near the ground and the driving rain had reduced the visibility. When one of the locals heard me grumbling about being behind schedule, he said to me, "Georgie, it is better in this country to be down here wishing you were up there, than up there wishing you were down here." And of course, he was right, as many unlucky Alaskan air travelers have discovered.

In a few days, the weather cleared enough for the plane to land. I flew immediately to Cordova and from there to Seattle. The trip really opened my eyes about Alaska. Even at that time, expenses were high, and I spent considerably more money than I intended to. But I had long wanted to see this beautiful country and explore a few of its wild rivers. I considered the trip worth the expense.

A couple of years later, I flew over much of Alaska trying to find additional rivers to explore by raft. I flew over the Seward Peninsula, much of the interior, and finally up north across the Brooks Range. In the North Country from the air, at that time, you could see hundreds of oil barrels scattered across the landscape. The country there is somewhat smooth and rolling, and I decided the rivers were not worth running.

But just because I had decided not to explore other Alaskan rivers, it didn't mean that I had written off all the north country. For a number of years I had also been hearing about the tremendous rapids on the Fraser River, the Big Bend of the Columbia River of British Columbia, and the Nahanni in the Northwest Territories. Rumor had it that some of these rivers were almost impassable to rafts. I had by now learned that local rapid stories often have no basis in fact. For some reason, local people often picture nearby wild rivers as much worse than they really are. I feel that, in most cases, since no one has actually run these rivers from one end to the other, that the size of the unknown rapids lying deep in the interior gets blown all out of proportion.

That summer I first planned to run the Columbia at the Big Bend, then take the boats out at Revelstoke, truck them over to Golden, run the Fraser, tackling Hell's Gate Rapid in the process.

When we reached Big Bend of the Columbia just out of Golden, British Columbia, I encountered my first obstacle. The highway here ran high above the water. My problem was how to get these rafts safely down to the water, since none of the river rats was due until the next day. I thought I'd roll them down that steep slope, but I was afraid they would drop into the water at the bottom. Just then, a bystander volunteered to hike down and stop the rafts. Since I needed help, I decided to let him stop the rafts if necessary. The rafts quit rolling, however, long before they reached the river.

I was told to expect Surprise Rapids, Gordon Rapids, Twelve-Mile Rapid, Priest Rapid, Death Rapid and others. Priest Rapid gave us the most challenge. It contained a few large rocks and a drop of about two feet, but in the big boat which I had taken because I intended to run Hell's Gate in it, we went through almost without getting wet. Truthfully, I can say that I ran this portion of the river for a full five days without encountering anything I would call a real rapid.

A passenger from Chicago asked if he could bring his kayak. I had room on the big barge so I agreed. He wanted to run the fast water above Revelstoke. That last day he started down river before we were ready to leave in the big raft. That was the last we saw of him for eight hours. As we were deflating the rafts that night at Revelstoke, he suddenly came walking across a bridge.

"Just after I left," he said, "a whirlpool caught me. I was afraid to stay with the kayak, so I jumped out, swam to the shore, crawled up to the highway and hitchhiked here."

"I know water," I told him. "We'll probably find it in the log jam at the mill downstream."

"I hope he doesn't find it," his wife said aside to me. "I don't want our children to lose a father."

I called ahead to the mill, however, and asked them to look for the kayak. Sure enough they found it in a log jam and the next day he had it back.

We then took the boats out at Revelstoke, put them on a truck and drove them to British Columbia. We would enter the Thompson here, join the Fraser, and tackle Hell's Gate. No one had run Hell's Gate on this river for at least forty years. And before that, only four people had gone through the rapids and lived.

At Kamloops, many of the townspeople urged us to reconsider. That rapid, they told us, was impassable, and we were going to take thirteen people. The news that we intended to tackle Hell's Gate made front page news all over British Columbia and a number of reporters showed up to interview us at Kamloops.

I offered to take any of them who wanted to go on the trip. But only the Vancouver Sun reporter accepted this challenge.

"Georgie, are you sure you'll make Hell's Gate without difficulty?" he asked. "After all, it's a ferocious rapid."

"Yes," I said. "I'll make it."

"Okay," he said. "I'll file my story before we leave. If I wait until we take the raft out, the other papers will scoop me."

The water on the Fraser was fast, but until we reached Hell's Gate, we encountered very few big rapids. One passenger had brought a book which described all the rapids on the Fraser River. Every night he would read to us about the horrors that we would encounter the next day. Then the next day, we would find almost nothing. I'm afraid I just never get used to this kind of exaggeration.

Finally, we came to Hell's Gate itself. Now I have to admit no one exaggerated the danger. That water (almost 125,000 cubic feet per second) shot through that 110-foot wide, man-made gorge with all the speed of an express train. In addition, just beyond lay a huge black rotating whirlpool that looked capable of swallowing an oil barge.

Several weeks before running this river, I had driven to Hell's Gate to examine the rapid in detail. I knew its reputation and I wanted to make sure I really could get through. One arm of the current shot downstream just skimming the whirlpool. The other arm came directly out from a sheer rock wall on the left. I reasoned that if I applied power at just the right time and headed into the wall, one current would take me into the other and I would ride safely through the rapid without too much danger.

If I powered too early, I would hit above the wall and swing around into the whirlpool. If I powered too late, I would already be in the whirlpool. The whirlpool itself couldn't sink my huge raft, but if I got in there with those giant bundles of logs that the loggers were constantly sending downriver, then I would be in trouble.

And now we were approaching Hell's Gate. Whenever I run a rapid like this, I never stop just before going through. I already have a general idea of what I intend to do. And conditions change so rapidly that I want to make decisions right at the moment. In running any rapid, there is always one place where you must act. Miss that moment and you are in trouble immediately.

Now the river began to narrow; the

This is Hell's Gate on the Fraser River in British Columbia, where people drive down to the cliff's edge to watch.

water picked up speed. Just below I could see a cauldron of white froth boiling skyward. Suddenly we shot over the brink and down. I waited . . . one . . . two . . . three. Now I gave it full power right into that sheer rock wall. Then as the wave swept over me, I lifted the motor out of the water. The current caught me; that huge raft balanced like a ballet dancer within feet of the whirlpool. I was drenched with sweat. Then as the momentum carried me through to the deeper water below, I knew we had it made.

Somehow, when things come off so perfectly like this, I find it hard to believe it isn't preordained. So many things could happen to throw us off in one of those rapids, yet my luck in the really crucial moments always seems to hold.

When we had finished loading the rafts on the truck, someone came running up with a newspaper. The headlines proclaimed: "River Rats Conquer Hell's Gate."

We were celebrities. You should have seen the smile on the faces of those two Canadians. They were heroes and they went around patting each other on the back.

Today, commercial Canadian river runners operate on the Fraser on a regular basis. But at that time, no one had taken a group like ours through Hell's Gate; I could count another first.

After successfully running what I considered to be the only really interesting rivers in Southern Canada, I once again turned my attention north. For my next conquest, the South Nahanni River in the Northwest Territories seemed like a good bet. Rutor had it that Virginia Falls (on the upper South Nahanni), where we would start, was twice as high as Niagara Falls. Also, if the rumor was true, we would encounter some good rapids below the falls.

I really liked the idea of running the South Nahanni since it would give me a chance to explore a fascinating area I had never been in before. The river rises out of the nine-thousand-foot-high Mackenzie Mountains lying along the border of the Yukon and the Northwest Territories, and from there traverses a gigantic land of high mountains, forests, animals, lakes, swamps, and sand plains.

After thinking about this trip for some time I began working out the details by mail. My people, I found, could reach Waston Lake, in the Yukon, by either bus or commercial airline. From there I was able to charter float planes to fly us northeast to the South Nahanni River.

On July 30, I put the rafts and motors on a plane in Los Angeles, then I drove north by truck to the Canadian Border and from there to Dawson Creek and on up the Alcan Highway to Watson Lake, which was a distance of almost 2400 miles. At Watson Lake I met my twelve river rats who had just arrived from all over the United States. The trip had attracted men and women ranging in age from eighteen to their late seventies. I love mixtures like this.

Mining activity in Canada at this time was at a fever pitch and mining traffic had precedent over other transportation uses. As a result, I had to wait several days until they could make a pontoon plane available.

The rafts I had shipped from Los Angeles had not yet arrived. I was now becoming anxious since I was scheduled to go directly from there to Guatemala. Any delays on one end would make me late on the other. I could just visualize ten or twelve river rats waiting in Guatemala while I was still running rivers in the Northwest Territories. It wasn't a comforting picture. I had, however, learned on my many trips to Mexico that I frequently run into delays and I must learn to wait.

On our third day at Watson Lake, a pontoon plane became available and the company wanted to start flying us in to Virginia Falls. I hesitated. My rafts still hadn't arrived, but if I didn't take advantage of the plane when I had it, I might have to wait even longer. So I decided to start my river rats into the river.

On the first trip the plane touched down for a landing on the river near a small rocky island and smacked a pontoon on some overhanging bushes. The pilot didn't think it was too bad at the time but after looking it over back in Watson Lake, he decided he'd damaged a strut. He said, "I'm not going to take a fully loaded plane back in there, Georgie. It's too dangerous. I can, however, land on a straight part of the river just above the falls, then ferry your people back."

That left me in a predicament. Most of my river rats were several hundred miles northeast on a small island and here I was stuck in Watson Lake without my boats and motors. I couldn't seem to get any information out of the local airline officials. For all I knew, everything was sitting at an airport somewhere between here and Los Angeles.

Fortunately the rafts and motors arrived the next morning. Two hours later, I was headed north. I had heard Virginia Falls were spectacular. That huge mass of falling water must have dropped at least 400 feet—in the middle, high chimneys of rock rose above the water surface separating the falls into two channels which joined below.

We flew over the falls, then the pilot circled and set down on what appeared, from that vantage point, to be a wide, placid lake. It was so peaceful and serene that if I hadn't known the falls were just around the corner I wouldn't have believed it.

After dropping me, the pilot made the short hop upriver to the island and brought back my river rats. Now that I had everyone together I breathed easier.

Unfortunately, we weren't out of the woods yet, and that's no pun. In order to start down the river, I would have to portage my heavy rafts and equipment around the falls.

Luckily, two young high school football players had come on the trip. Ironically, I had almost turned down their applications. I had received a letter from their parents originally asking if two seventeen-year-old boys could make the trip. I replied that they weren't old enough to travel by themselves. The parents wrote back and said the boys traveled alone extensively and really wanted to go on this trip. They also said they, the parents, would take complete responsibility. Finally I agreed. Now the boys were here with me and eager to start portaging those heavy motors down that steep hillside to the bottom of the falls.

Before I let them or anyone start to the bottom with the equipment, however, I had to find a safe way to the bottom. I don't think I've ever seen such a dense thicket of small trees as there was near the top of that falls. The bottom part opened up somewhat, but dropped steeply into the canyon down a pathway that was half creek bed, half slime. At the last steep drop someone had anchored logs crosswise to form rickety steps.

To get down, I had to force my way through muskeg and broken branches; thorns tore at my clothes; deerflies and mosquitoes stung my face and hands. It was miserable. Wading through that muskeg was like wading through a pile of wet pillows. Even with the oozing mud sucking my boots off my feet I somehow managed to make my way down to the bottom of the slope and mark the trail as I went along with yellow crepe paper.

This was a trick I had learned earlier in the Grand Canyon. If I need to retrace my steps or want to leave a trail for someone to follow, I mark it with yellow crepe paper. It could be seen from long distances and I could easily pick it up as I leave.

Back at the top, the two boys cut a couple of poles from two small trees, lashed one motor between these and began to inch their way down the marked trail. Getting those motors through the dense thicket of trees at the top proved extremely difficult. Large broken branches impeded their progress, and little by little, the boys inched their way to the bottom. Then huffing and puffing, they came back to help the rest of us with the rafts. I really had to admire their stamina and spirit. I was also extremely thankful at that point that I had changed my mind and let them come.

Everyone, of course, took care of getting his own personal equipment down the trail. Two older sisters, Marjorie Steurt and Frances McIver, who must have been at least seventy years old, had also come on this trip with me.

People often tell me that I'm crazy to take older women on these rugged trips. I've found, however, that many of them have that old-time pioneer spirit that just doesn't seem to exist anymore. These women don't mind hard work under extremely adverse conditions. They can, for instance, go all day in a driving rain without complaining, or undergo severe hardship and come up smiling. They also know how to wait many hours without becoming bored. That's the way Marjorie and Frances were.

I could have asked someone else to carry their heavy neoprene packs to the bottom, but they insisted on doing it themselves. Naturally they couldn't handle the sixty pounds all at once so they took the packs apart and made three trips.

I'll never forget the sight of those two women struggling up and down that steep slope. Every step they took, the mud and goo clung to their shoes. Caked mud covered their clothes from head to foot and the sweat gleamed on their faces.

Several of us managed to wrestle the two-hundred-fifty-pound rafts down to the top part through the trees, then when we came to the steep rocky part we simply turned them loose and let them roll to the bottom. It took many trips to get everything below the falls. As far as I have been able to learn, this was the heaviest, biggest portage ever conducted by river runners up to this point.

We had to portage the motors around Virginia Falls, despite steep slopes and trees. We then shoved off down the South Fork of the Nahanni River and wound through Headless Valley.

By the time we assembled the equipment, supplies and river rats at the bottom of the falls ready to go it was the second day of portaging and I was absolutely exhausted. Of course I had long ago come to realize that in any wilderness situation I am likely to run into unexpected trouble, so I am always ready. In addition, all my life I have believed that fate is with me no matter what I encounter. Whenever I run into a problem like this, I simply relax and work it out.

During the day-and-a-half of portaging,

heavy rain plagued us at intervals. On the second day I managed to blow up the rafts during the morning, then right after lunch we shoved off down the river.

The first few miles we ran a number of mild rapids, then we swung around a bend to catch the full force of several high-cross waves. The river here slammed into a cliff, then poured to the right. As the boat shot sideways on these high waves, the motor roared, then roared again. For what seemed like an eternity we hung motionless in that seething water, then suddenly we dropped to the level of the river and went racking downstream.

Below this several miles, a large whirlpool grabbed us, and began to suck the raft down low in the water like an octopus that had its tentacles hooked on both sides of the boat and was pulling us down with all its might. The water gurgled threateningly, and began to slosh over the side. Then all at once, the whirlpool released us and once again we were hurtling along with the current.

These encounters were exciting, but nothing like the rapids of the Colorado River—perhaps. The ones I had heard about were farther on downriver. I waited, expectantly, looking for giant rapids around every bend.

Then, about thirty miles below Virginia Falls, we ran through a series of strangely spectacular canyons. Just below the junction of the Flat River and the Nahanni, the banks began to close in and the stream soon roared between two towering rock walls. At the beginning of the second canyon, we encountered a feature called "The Gate." The river here turns in a sharp S-curve between high cliffs, and ahead I could see a tall rock pinnacle outlined against a very blue sky.

Between the second and first canyons we passed through ten-mile-long "Headless Valley." The name, I am told, was attached to this whole area after William and Frank McLeod ventured into the valley looking for gold in the early 1900s. Their headless bodies were discovered here shortly afterwards. Several years later, another body appeared here, also headless.

This created a sensation; the natives claimed that ghosts were out to kill anyone who entered their valley. North Country inhabitants said the Indians did it. Others felt that rival trappers and miners killed the men. After that, until we ran the river through this section, only fifteen or twenty people had visited the region— most were never heard from again.

As a result, an air of mystery hangs over the valley, and many of the local residents refuse to even go near. Some newspapers played it up as a valley of death where murder and pestilence run rampant. One story had it that it was impossible to enter the valley and live. I'm afraid I don't have much faith in mystery stories, but I don't believe the government line, either, which goes something like this:

Undoubtedly, several people have lost their lives in the region, but fatalities of this nature can always be expected in remote districts when adequate preparation, including provision of sufficient food, has not been made. It is reasonable to believe that some deaths in the South Nahanni have resulted from drowning or starvation. In such cases, the bodies of the deceased would have been devoured by predatory animals.

Whatever the case, I wasn't really concerned, but several of the trip members began to feel quite apprehensive. One told me—as a joke, I hope—that if he lost his head here he wanted the rest of his body shipped home to be buried in the family plot.

It took several hours to raft through, then at the far end we entered the most spectacular of the three canyons, where the gray rock walls rose sheer some 1500 feet high. I marveled that a river the size of the Nahanni could find passage through such a cleft.

Beyond the first valley we came to the second hot springs on the river where Gus Krous's cabin was. This unusual man has lived here for fifty years and was, beside one other prospector, the river's only inhabitant. We camped below the Krous cabin; it had bushes growing out of the roof. We had long talks with Gus and his Indian wife about life in the Canadian wilderness. I kept wondering why anyone would want to spend his life in this remote Canadian valley, but I'm sure Gus probably wondered why I spent so much of my life exploring rivers and running wild rapids.

Before we left, the group tried out the hot sulphur springs here. What wonderful warm water after the icy Nahanni! After a few of our party walked around in it, however, the hot springs turned into liquid mud, and I came out dirtier than when I went in.

As we came down lower on the Nahanni River, we began to see Indians along the bank. Sometimes, we would sweep around a bend and see a group of four or five fishing in the ripples. Other times, we would find women washing clothes on the rocks. We didn't see any villages, but I hear that enough Indians live along the river during the summer that they land planes at certain places to bring in supplies. Nowhere did we find anything I would call a rapid and I was extremely disappointed.

In the lower reaches, the South Nahanni meanders along many channels in an extremely flat monotonous valley. I was never really sure which channel to pick, but I fell back on my San Juan River experience and let the motor pick the channel. Fortunately, the motor always seemed to choose the right channel, and on the fifth day we reached the wide, swift Liard River.

Throughout this entire section it was blazing hot in the daytime and bitterly cold at night. The nights reminded me of my November trip long ago—with Harry Aleson in Cataract Canyon. At night I just couldn't seem to get warm.

Finally, the Liard joined the MacKenzie, which was as big as a lake. We could hardly see from one side to the other. It was also drizzling again—something we had come to expect most of the time in the North Country.

On the second day after we entered the McKenzie River, we reached a small settlement, Fort Simpson, where ocean-going vessels come down the river from the Arctic Ocean. I had been told that two planes a week landed here, so I had speeded up the trip to make sure I arrived by Tuesday. Fort Simpson, I discovered, was serviced by only one plane a week, so we had to wait three days. Time was squeezing me again because of the Guatemala trip. I also worried that I would get bumped on the next flight by mining traffic. Fortunately, I managed to get out on the next flight and reached Guatemala in time to meet my river rats.

I had enjoyed the scenery along the South Nahanni and I was delighted to finally be able to explore the Northwest Territories for the first time. The rapids had been a disappointment. I now understood that I can't always believe the rumors and that people often invent rapids that just don't exist.

One of the other surprises that I had on the North Country trip was the fact that more women than men went with me. This is in contrast to Mexican trips where few women show up.

In the north, it rains; the cold became almost unbearable. And the mosquitoes and flies drive us crazy. But the women like it. I've often wondered if they haven't heard about the lack of women in this area, and have some fanciful idea about finding a husband there. I have no way to verify this; it's only my theory.

I haven't taken a trip here to Canada for several years now. I don't have any plans for any more North Country exploration. The country, however, is big, wild and lonely . . . and I can honestly say that never for one moment, not even when I was in the middle of portaging Virginia Falls, did I ever regret the efforts in exploring the North Country. It is truly our last great wilderness. It is with much regret that I watched the pipeline being built in Alaska, and the wilderness of Canada being opened to man. For, like the rest of the United States and Mexico, with progress will come the dams, and with the dams, the really good wild water will be lost forever.

The end of the first trip down the Copper River.

White Water Adventure – A Mexican Specialty

I had been running the white water of the Colorado, the Snake, the Salmon and other rivers for many years before I turned my attention south of the Mexican border. Looking back now I realize that I needed those early years to give me the experience necessary to handle the unexpected dangers that I was bound to encounter there. By the late 1950s I had begun to consider exploring the rivers of Mexico and South America.

At this time I had never been to Mexico and I really didn't know what to expect from any of the rivers. I guessed that somebody else had explored them at length. That turned out to be a false assumption. Up to that time no one had paid much attention to the inaccessible sections of Mexico's wild rivers.

Except for the Indian myths and an occasional report from a jungle party, the Mexican officials knew nothing about what lay in the depths of those deep canyons. On our Rio Grande de Santiago trip, for instance, the Mexican army engineers had no idea where the old dams and waterfalls were located and eagerly requested that I give them a full report when I returned. It seemed strange to me at the time that the government officials knew so little about their own country, but as I discovered later, the miners and back-country villagers simply built dams wherever they needed them, and in most cases no official group had explored any of the rivers to find out just what did exist.

On most of the Mexican rivers that I eventually explored I was literally the first person to run that water and live to tell about it.

Being first made Mexican river exploration all the more intriguing to me. After I developed special boats and techniques for running rapids, of course, it really wasn't such a big deal anymore, yet it always gave me a feeling of accomplishment I couldn't obtain any other way.

Over the years I've decided that there are really only four Mexican rivers worth running: the Upper Balsas, which runs from south of Mexico City west toward the Pacific Ocean; the Rio Grande de Santiago, originating in Lago de Chapala near Guadalajara and draining toward the Pacific; the Rio Grijalva, rising in the mountains of Guatemala and emptying into the Gulf of Mexico; and the Usumancinta, running along the border between Mexico and Guatemala. All of these rivers, except the Usumacinta, have tremendous rapids, traverse spectacular country, and run for miles through deep isolated gorges. The tropical scenery surrounding all four rivers makes them especially intriguing. The jungle here contains plush bamboo, wild tobacco, brilliantly colored flowers, including orchids, and a wide variety of birds.

Beside the scenic beauty all these rivers have the added hazards of crocodiles and poisonous snakes. The natives along the river banks tell blood-curdling tales of people bitten in two by the crocodiles or paralyzed for life by the snakes. Most of these stories, of course, are gross exaggerations. Back home on the Grand Canyon I also hear horror stories about the rattlesnake, but in all my years there I don't think I've ever seen anyone bitten. Although we've seen numerous crocodiles and snakes on the Mexican trips, they've never given us a bit of trouble.

Whenever we run a Mexican river we are nearly always treated like royalty by the back-country villagers. When we ran the Rio Grande de Santiago for the first time, for instance, hundreds of people and dogs came to say goodbye. (I had the feeling at the time, however, that they expected to see us dashed to pieces on the first rapid.)

In this village as in most others in the Mexican back country the men and boys there to see us off gathered in one group, the women and children in another. This division occurs at almost every festive occasion. Also, only Mexican men come to the parties. I really never pay much attention to whether my river rats are men or women since we're generally one big group without regard to sex. I suppose that's why the Mexican custom seems strange to me. But I will say that all the people in our entire party, men and women alike, are always accepted there with open arms.

This Mexican hospitality takes a number of different forms. At the primitive settlement of Paso de La Yesa, an excited group of Mexicans crowded around when we landed, inspected the rafts thoroughly, then invited us into their homes for tequila. This seems to be one of those rituals

I was the first person to explore many Mexican rivers by raft. The Mexicans were at first skeptical, and often told exaggerated stories of the huge rapids that lay downstream.

we run into everywhere in the Mexican bush. The villagers can't get beer or other liquor easily because most supplies come in by burro back or plane. They do, however, make their own tequila, which flows like water. I'm not quite sure how it's made but it's one of the worst brews I think I've ever tasted. I don't care for it at all. It's pretty hard to turn down a drink when your host thinks he's offering you a real treat. But we do try to drink as little as possible.

Although I didn't really care for this kind of tequila I do enjoy the Mexican beer whenever we can find it. We've discovered that Germans in Mexico always have beer regardless of the transportation difficulties, and that Mexican mines nearly always have German partners. As a result we always keep an eagle eye out for mines along the river since it means a beer stop. I find Mexican beer especially refreshing; so on my trips I make a big thing out of looking for beer on the river. In one case we hadn't had a beer for five days. Coming around a bend we spotted a small mine and headed in. The Mexicans on the dock saw me run the boats in and knew I was in charge, so when I pulled up they looked at me and said, "Cervesa?"

I answered, "Cervesa!" And they handed me a beer.

By this time everyone was really drooling, but I decided to have some fun with them so I just stood there and drank the beer, smacking my lips with each sip. When I finished, I said, "Okay, now give them some."

What a hub-bub! I thought for a minute they were going to throw me overboard, but they just left me standing there looking silly, and dove for the beer themselves.

Often in the Mexican back country our reception becomes even more personal than this. On the Grijalva, for instance, when we were overtaken by a cloudburst, a local farmer immediately invited all nine of us to share a roof with him, his wife, and their five children. When we gratefully accepted, he swept the dirt floor and kicked out four pigs, three dogs, and a number of chickens so we could spread out our sleeping bags. During the night the pigs kept banging the door to get back in, extremely upset that we had taken their sleeping quarters. Then, just as we were about to drop off to sleep, in popped six neighbors to throw a noisy party.

In yet another village, when we needed medical supplies, the jungle dentist simply locked his door and volunteered to guide us to the next village where we could find the necessary items. Delighted, we accepted and took off cross-country confidently led by the dentist, still wearing his white jacket. After a couple of hours we realized our guide was lost and under questioning he admitted he knew nothing about our route. In fact, he had never been that way before. That night he kept climbing trees to find a fire or a light to show him the way. We never did reach the next village or obtain our medical supplies, but at least our friend's heart was in the right place.

Often the back-country natives will throw a party at the drop of a hat. On one trip I had been forced to abandon our rafts, and the nearby villagers cut them apart to use the rubber for shoe soles and other essentials. They had, however, left one piece with the name "Georgie" on it face up in the sand. Next trip down when we pulled in at one of the silver mines, the workers suddenly gasped, pointed at the name "Georgie" on my boats and began talking excitedly in Spanish, and they insisted on throwing a party for us at the mine that evening.

What a bash! I knew how to square dance pretty well, so I faked it, and danced every one of those Mexican dances, really hamming it up. They seemed to love it.

Somehow during that evening the Mexicans decided that each member of our party must do something special. Our people loved it and did things they'd be too embarrassed to do back home. One fellow, for instance, put on a fancy elephant walk; another paraded around the room on his hands. One of our group, a young fellow named George, didn't seem too happy with the idea of performing. In fact as it came closer to his turn I could see he was visibly shaking.

"I can't do it, Georgie," he blurted out suddenly. "I don't know how to do anything."

"Sure you can," I told him. "You'll think of something."

"Hey," I said suddenly, "remember how you pitched beer cans in a bucket the other day? Well, pick up that cardboard box over there and when it comes your turn I'll toss in a few beer cans to start it off."

He seemed unsure but finally agreed to give it a try. Well, they started to play music for his turn and George started to weave back and forth with his box while I tossed in a couple of cans. All of a sudden the Mexican boys let out a big whoop and

began tossing beer cans at the box, faster and faster. Was he a hit! He kept catching them for about five minutes, then finally stopped, completely exhausted. The party itself continued until the wee hours of the next morning. I'm not sure how we made it out on the river the next day, but the whole group loved the experience and George will undoubtedly remember that party for the rest of his life.

Besides the warm feeling I have for these Mexican villagers, I've also over the years developed a real sense of admiration for the Mexican bush pilots. These heroic flyers just don't seem to feel any sense of danger. They take chances that most American pilots wouldn't think of taking, land in places that would scare me to death, and fly aircraft that look like it won't get off the ground.

The first time we ran the Grijalva River, for instance, and wanted to survey our route by air, Marshall Bond and I rented the most decrepit looking Cesna I've ever seen. Its only recommendation was that it was warmed up and ready to go when we were. Over the river the pilot shouted, "For fifty pesos more I'll take you down into the gorge so you can really look over the river."

Marshall glanced down, shuddered and shouted back, "No way!"

The pilot looked at me, saw my face, laughed, and said, "We'll do it anyway, Señora."

Down we went hundreds of feet below the top. The plane rolled and twisted around the sharp corners missing the cliffs by feet. Coming to the end of the canyon the pilot pulled the nose back abruptly and shot over the edge in a steep climb. When

These shots are from a Rio Grande de Santiago trip— the thatched huts on stilts line the lower parts of the river, and the entire village comes out to greet us.

he had climbed several hundred feet more he waggled his wings at the river, gave me a toothy grin, and headed back for Guadalajara.

Despite their hair-raising ways of flying, these pilots have gotten me out of trouble several times, and I still make a preliminary flight over every river I intend to run since it gives me some idea of what I'll be up against. I do this even if I've gone down a river several times before, since conditions are never the same from one trip to the next.

My first real Mexican white water exploration actually took place in late summer and fall of 1958. The year before, I spent two weeks looking for possible rivers to run. I drove to Mexico, then rented a plane at Chihuahua, and partially explored the Rio Yaqui. This river runs through a four-thousand-foot-deep canyon and looks extremely exciting from the air. When I returned home I had made up my mind to give the Rio Yaqui a try the following year.

These early Mexican exploratory trips of the late 1950s coincided almost exactly with dam development in Mexico. During the most active building years it wasn't at all uncommon for me to run a river one season, then come back the next year and find that river completely changed.

These Mexican dams, both new and old, have caused me more trouble in Mexico than anything else. On that very first river trip in 1958, a hidden dam built to supply hydro-electric power for a nearby mine almost proved my undoing. Actually I'm not sure why I or one of my party hasn't been killed in Mexico, but I've decided that luck is really on my side, at least for now.

By the time I had decided to go ahead with the 1958 trip I knew pretty well how I intended to tackle the Mexican rivers. I decided that the smaller ten-man boats lashed together my way would give me the needed flexibility.

I also picked my first party carefully. By this time Orville Miller, the long, lean professor, had become my right-hand man. Orville was extremely skillful in white water, knew Spanish, and could always be counted on in an emergency. The other four who made that first trip with me, including one woman, Lillian Lasch, had considerable white water experience. I feel that every expedition of this type should have at least one member with a real sense of humor, to help relieve the tension. Ours was Marshall Bond, Jr., who had explored Mexico with me the year before and who had run the Colorado River was me several times. He had a habit of just blurting out whatever he was thinking. Most of the time he really broke me up. He also did crazy things. On one trip, for instance, he brought along a small spray can labeled

Crocodile Repellent; another time in Tuxutal, he lit candles for us and when I asked why, he said it was the native custom to light candles for those who wouldn't return from the river.

On that first trip to Mexico I had no real idea what kind of permission I needed to run the Mexican rivers. I look back now and realize I was terribly naive in those days. I decided that first year that I'd simply ask everybody to secure Mexican visas, then I'd just charter a plane, load the rafts and supplies on board and head for Mexico.

With a little effort I found a Mexican charter outfit at the Riverside Airport that agreed to fly us in their Beechcraft Bonanza. I paid their fee by check and got ready to go. On September 21 the six of us simply showed up at the airport. Our rafts and other equipment had already been shipped to Nogales, Mexico.

"I can't fly you," the pilot told me. "My partner took off with all your money." He then refused to leave the ground until I paid again—cash this time, no checks.

What a pickle! I needed every penny I had on me for Mexico and there was no one around to cash a check. Then I remembered a nearby friend who had once said, "Georgie, if you ever need help, just call." I got him on the phone and immediately blurted out, "Bring me a thousand dollars." Thirty minutes later he showed up with the cash. I paid the pilot and we piled in.

We were now headed for Hermosillo, Central Sonora, Mexico. Here I intended to pass through customs, then fly to a landing strip near the Rio Yaqui. We had explored this river the year before by air and it looked exciting. As we approached Mexico the plane began to bounce up and down sickeningly. The clouds turned dark and ominous. By the time we crossed the border we were in the middle of one of the worst storms I had ever seen.

When it came time to land in Hermosillo we could see nothing out there in the vast Sonora wilderness but empty canyons and forbidding hills stretching to the horizon. Finally, with our gas running low, the pilot swung back toward an emergency landing strip on the coast at Bha Kio. I hadn't been too concerned up to this point, but when I spotted that Bha Kio strip I caught my breath. It looked like a giant sea of mud. I knew we could never make a landing there.

"There's just enough gas for ten minutes more," the pilot told me. I squirmed in my seat.

"That road," he said, pointing down to a paved highway running from the coast. "We'll land there." With that he dropped a wing sharply and almost dove toward the ground.

Just then I glanced across at Marshall Bond. In a quavering voice he was repeating over and over, "I wish I'd took a bus. I wish I'd took a bus."

"Say that one more time," I told him, "and I'll shove you out that door myself."

Then the wheels touched, we sped along the pavement for what seemed an eternity, then bumped gingerly to a stop. I heaved a sigh of relief and scrambled out the door. There, directly in front of us, stood a sign in Spanish: *Stop, Bridge Out.* Three hundred feet more and that would have been the end. I suppose I should

have been frightened on this occasion but I've always felt that when my time came it came, so these adventures never bothered me. Once they're over I'm always ready for the next one.

After landing we had to find gasoline, so the pilot and several of our party set out on foot across the damaged bridge and down the road. Two hours later they were back with the gasoline sloshing in open buckets. Somehow they managed to pour it in the plane's tanks without a funnel. We then took off down the middle of the highway and landed a few hours later in Hermosillo.

That year Mexico was having its worst flood season in years and the pilots at the Hermosillo Airport convinced us we just couldn't land on the strip near the Rio Yaqui.

We decided at that point to change our plans, fly instead to Guadalajara and tackle the Rio Grande de Santiago. I had heard this river had good rapids and had it in mind either as an alternative to the Rio Yaqui or for a trip the following year.

When we got in the air, however, and saw the damage the flood waters had done, I had my doubts that any of the Mexican rivers would be navigable by raft that season. As we headed south I crossed my fingers and hoped we'd find the situation different along the Rio Grande de Santiago. When we flew over the river a few hours later I was pleasantly surprised. It looked tremendous, with fine, unflooded campsites, and good swift rapids.

Once we saw we could run the river here without difficulty we decided to land at Guadalajara nearby and rent a truck to bring us back to a river launching site.

When we checked into a Guadalajara hotel a few hours later I felt very apprehensive. I hadn't intended to go anywhere near a city on this trip so I had only brought along nylon coveralls. They were great for running rapids, and beating around in the Mexican brush but not so good for city wear. In addition I had heard the Mexicans didn't want you in the hotels unless you're dressed up.

"Don't worry, Georgie," my friends told me. "As long as you have money you'll be welcome."

This proved to be true. In fact the owner of the hotel not only made sure we felt welcome but personally took a hand in helping us secure the necessary permits from the Marine Department and the Commission of Electricity. This, of course, was a disadvantage of coming into one of the larger cities. We ran into far more red tape there than we did in the outlying areas. It only took a couple of days to clear up the details, however; then we rented a truck and headed for the river.

Unfortunately when the pilot flew back and brought my rafts from Nogales, he had brought only two of my three. This meant I had to run without the usual three-boat combination.

When we reached our jumping-off point I was delighted to see some really high water. I had run big water like this for many years on the Colorado River and loved it. Over the next few days we ran a succession of large rapids that convinced me the Rio Grande de Santiago had a slightly greater drop than the Colorado. The trip up to this point, while enjoyable, had presented no real danger.

That afternoon we encountered some really rough water with big rapids, huge boulders, and many blind corners. At the bottom of that section we swung into a stretch of deceptively calm water that caught us completely off guard. We could see far downriver and it looked extremely peaceful. Since it looked safe enough for awhile, we sprawled all over the rafts and just drifted with the current. A mile later I caught movement out of the corner of my eye. Startled, I realized that two excited Mexicans were racing along the bank, shouting and waving their arms frantically. Lillian stood up and gasped, "Georgie, there's a dam ahead!"

I swung the raft abruptly while the others sprang for the oars and we bumped to a landing in a grove of bananas scarcely a hundred yards above the drop. It was a dam all right. A thirty-foot-high dam built in 1907 to supply electricity for a local silver mine. I just stood there and shook my head. This was one of those dams the Mexican engineers knew nothing about. A few hundred yards more and they would have been fishing dead river runners out of the water.

We then hired a gang of workers from the hydroelectric plant to help us portage our gear and by late afternoon we had the raft reassembled and camp set up on a ledge below the dam. From there the river alternated between fierce rapids and wider calm stretches providing us with glimpses of native life along the Rio Grande de Santiago which included mules ferried across the river on cable strung high above the water, dugout canoes occupied by naked young men who seemed delighted to see us, and thatched houses on stilts bearing a great resemblance to those found

A crowd of well-wishers watched as we raced under the Pan American Highway into the jaws of El Sumidero—our destination, seen from above.

all over the Pacific and Southwest Asia.

On the lower stretch below the dam I managed to break a propeller and the drive shaft gears of the motor on a hidden rock, forcing us to row the rapids the rest of the trip. Limping along in this manner we finished the trip four days later in Santiago Ixquintla, then headed back for the Guadalajara airport and the States.

Each year after this for several years I tried to explore a different Mexican river. In 1960 I decided to try the seven-hundred-mile Rio Balsas, Mexico's longest river. This trip presented a few problems, as do most of my exploratory trips, but nothing like the ones I encountered later in Mexico.

On this trip, after looking at a map, I decided to enter the Rio Balsas near Ixcamilpa, south of Mexico City, in later August and hired a truck driver who said he knew exactly where to take us. What a mistake hiring that guy was! By this time I should have become wise to the ways of Mexican truck drivers, but in those days I just never seemed to learn.

The first few hours on the road were great fun. We explored the town of Cualta. From there we turned off the pavement and within an hour the truck became lodged in nearly impassable ruts. At this point the driver kept muttering to himself about crazy *gringos*.

About an hour later I realized that he

was lost and when I questioned him he admitted he had never been in that part of Mexico before. I don't often become angry on river trips but at that point, I could have strangled him.

Fortunately, within a few minutes, a truck came along headed in the opposite direction. I flagged down the driver who just stared at me when he heard our story.

"Only a footpath goes to Ixcamilpa," he told us. "You can't get there by truck."

No road! I stood there stunned. Just how would we get to the river? Then I remembered when I had explored the Upper Balsas by plane I had seen a tributary that crossed the paved Pan American Highway that wouldn't take us too far out of the way. All we had to do was to drive back to the highway and take a short detour from there to the river.

Our Mexican driver grumbled about this, but agreed to drive us where we wanted to go. Finally, about midnight, we arrived at the crossing of the Rio Atayac and the Pan American Highway. It was raining again and we scrambled under a tarp in the back of the truck. The tarp provided absolutely no protection and the rain soaked all of us to the skin.

Next morning we shoved off downstream. The river was so narrow there I was forced to run single boats instead of the three-boat combination I usually use. We didn't find a single rapid along this stretch of the river but the setting was gorgeous. Orchids grew everywhere; bamboo grass reached ten feet, and the banks were lined with a small forest of wild tobacco plants. Strangely, the natives we passed stared at us in silence.

A short time later we rounded a bend and came on a small deserted village. The men, we discovered, were gone and the women and small children had fled to the woods when they saw us coming. We simply hung costume jewelry on the trees and crawled back in our rafts.

The next day was a different story. The villagers at San Juan del los Rios downstream were delighted to see us. We gave them costume jewelry and holy pictures. They gave us a tour of their village.

Below here the river began to narrow, the current became stronger and stronger, and suddenly downriver I could see a series of wild, hair-raising rapids. Since it was now almost dark I decided to wait until morning to tackle that turbulent water.

Next morning we shoved off shortly after dawn. At the first rapid the surging water roared over a flat rock and disappeared from sight. It was like taking a nose dive off a rooftop. The bottom fell out and suddenly we were hurtling from boulder to boulder down a steep narrow chute. Wham! An oar smashed on a rock. Wave after wave pounded the raft, then we floated free in calm water.

For the next several days we repeated this scene over and over. On the fifth day I discovered a ten-inch rip in the bottom of one of the boats and pulled into a sandbar to make repairs. One of my river rats jumped overboard to help and sunk knee deep in quicksand. We quickly grabbed him and hauled him back in the boat. Later I managed to make the repairs.

From there, the river grew calmer and on the sixth day we reached Coacalco, typical of the villages along this stretch of river. It had tile roofs, hard-packed dirt floors, corn storage cribs, and a historic old

The high point of our trip was Quechula where we found the jungle-covered ruin of a sixteenth century church which no North Americans had ever before visited.

church at the heart of the village. After that it was a calm float trip to our take-out point at Tuxtula, where the Acapulco Highway crosses the river. There I deflated the rafts, said goodbye to most of my people, and trucked the rafts back to Mexico City.

After this comparatively easy trip on the Rio Balsas, I'm afraid my Mexican trips got considerably rougher. By now the Mexicans were well into their new dam building program, and for the next several years every time I put a raft in the river I seemed to have trouble.

A good example of this occurred just a few years later on one of my exploratory trips to the Rio Grijalva. I had run this river previously and knew it contained some spectacular rapids and a narrow, tortuous gorge with nearly vertical cliffs that was called El Sumidero. The first time I tried this spectacular run, the head of the Mexican Tourist Bureau, Señor Camacho, had been positive the whole party would be killed, and made us sign a paper releasing the government from liability before allowing us to go ahead.

Actually the river in that area is extremely fierce. Little is known about that stretch of water and many myths and fears have grown up around it. Legend has it that two thousand Indians jumped off the high cliffs there during the days of Cortez. A lone explorer had lost his life just a month before our expedition. In addition, just before we arrived Señor Camacho had rescued a group of Mexican engineers who had lost a boat and most of their gear. Actually I didn't think we were taking unusual chances because I had learned long before how to run waters like these.

As far as I was concerned, El Sumidero, while exciting, was still just another series of rapids.

To watch out for us, Señor Camacho had placed six policemen along the canyon rim with orders to signal with rifle fire the minute anyone sighted us coming out of the rapids.

That first time, we launched the boats, ran for a few miles until the canyon narrowed, then pulled into the bank to see what we were facing. We climbed over a huge boulder and there before us the water was transformed from a lazy river into a boiling, smashing maelstrom of white water. The boulders here were at least the size of a house and the power of that water was tremendous. I decided, at that point, not to try it, but to portage around and reenter the river downstream.

With a great deal of difficulty, we hauled the boats upstream where we loaded them on a truck and drove to a village below El Sumidero.

In the meantime, the soldiers had been watching our progress from the canyon rim and, when they saw only one boat, had decided that our boats had broken apart and that we had all been killed. After that they began to watch for the bodies to float by.

We ran several small rapids below, then the roar of heavy water became louder and louder. And when the canyon narrowed I stopped to look at the rapid. This rapid appeared to be just as rough as the one we had portaged earlier, maybe worse. Only this time I couldn't go around; I had to run straight through.

I secured all the bags, then headed down the rapid. For a few minutes we bounced from one enormous hole to another, with the big heavy water pouring over us. Suddenly an explosive wave spun the boats, I raised the motor as high as I could, but it kept banging from one giant boulder to another. When we finally got through I discovered the motor was hanging by a slender thread and smashed beyond repair. I then unpacked the spare motor and ran the remaining miles to Villa Hermosa, where we took the boats out of the water.

*   *   *

Between the time of that first assault and this one the Mexican government had begun an ambitious hydroelectric project on a number of major rivers. Industrialization of this type is desperately needed to improve the Mexican economy. But dams also destroy wild rivers. And because of the Mexican dam building there are several formerly great rivers that I won't go near because the major rapids are under water. I knew that several dams were planned on the Grijalva, but I had been told that construction would not start until after we'd completed our trip and had returned to the United States. At this point eleven of us had been on the water several days without incident. Then at the end of the fourth day, we ran a series of exciting rapids then swung sharply around a bend to find a huge, half-completed earth dam blocking our way.

I sat there disappointed, looking at that giant mound of earth. I certainly didn't want to remove the boats here, because we'd have trouble getting permission to bring a truck down the dam road. What I

These pigs were part of the provisions that were poled upstream for the engineers working on the dam.

wanted to do was to find some way to bypass this dam so we could proceed on downriver. While these thoughts went through my mind, I noticed that although the earth dam lay directly across the river's path, that there was a half-full diversion tunnel at one side, half hidden by the construction work.

With a little luck we might find a way through it back to the river. I had no idea what lay ahead in the murky interior, nor for that matter, what we would find on the

147

other side. I did feel, however, that it might be worth a try. So I said to Orville, "Hike up there to the construction site and see if you can get permission to use the tunnel."

Grumbling, he set off up through the shale. When he disappeared over the top I wondered what kind of a reception he'd get. Fortunately for us, it was Sunday. Mexican red tape certainly is far worse than that found in the United States. Mexican officials can tie you up for days while they bounce you from one official to another. Sometimes it seems that everybody is afraid to take the responsibility.

Since this was Sunday, however, all Orville found at the top was one sleepy looking guard leaning on his gun. Orville pointed to us down on the river and explained as best he could in Spanish what we wanted to do. The guard just shrugged his shoulders, mumbled, "Help yourself," and turned away.

"Hey, Georgie," Orville said when he'd scampered back, "are we in luck! But we have to go today because tomorrow some official might get interested in us."

At that I got everybody together and moved the rafts right up to the face of the tunnel. I took one look and drew a long breath. The rafts hung over a good four inches on either side. "Boy," I said, "we're going to have a pretty tough time getting through there."

Orville just laughed and said, "Georgie, let's have a beer and maybe it'll look wider."

That seemed like a good idea even if it didn't change the tunnel, so we sat down and opened a beer.

Finally I said, "Okay, let's let some air out of each of the side rafts and see what happens." That's what we did and it gave us about six inches to spare.

After that we piled in and floated off into the dark. What an eerie feeling! I had at this point raised the motor because I had no idea what to expect in the darkness. Suddenly one of the girls screamed and the bottom dropped out. It's hard to tell how far we fell. It could have been two feet or six. It always seems farther in the darkness than it really is. A few minutes more and I could see light in the distance. Then we were on the river again. I grabbed my camera and began taking pictures of the tunnel. I planned to show this trip later on television and needed both the entrance and exit. I became so involved trying to get just the right shots that I had no idea what was happening around me.

"Rapid!" somebody shouted. "Rapid!"

I sat stunned for a second, then suddenly I threw the camera violently at the bottom of the boat and jumped toward the motor. There, right in front of us, loomed one of the biggest, roughest rapids I'd ever seen. The motor whirred, nothing . . . now it was too late . . . crack! an oar smashed on a rock leaving a ragged splintery stub. We didn't run that rapid; we just banged through. But a few minutes later we shot free into the calm water below.

Everybody came through shaken but unhurt. I rescued my camera from the bottom of the boat and resumed taking pictures. Shown later that winter those movies of our entrance and exit from the tunnel turned out to be quite spectacular.

While this may seem like a haphazard way to run a river, it's also part of the fun. There have been a number of deaths on the world's wild rivers from careless operation. I have, however, run rugged rapids thousands of times and have developed equipment and methods which make even the worst of them relatively safe. My boats turn in on each other, but they never turn over. If someone pitches out in the water they float down in their life jacket and we pick them up. As a result of this pre-planning and care I have never had an accidental death on any of my trips. This surprise rapid added to the enjoyment of the trip.

The next day we arrived at the village where I intended to leave the river. The rented truck was waiting so we loaded the boats and headed back to Guadalajara. With the tunnel episode as a warning, I guess I should have realized I was headed for a major disaster in Mexico, but until something actually happened I just wouldn't believe it.

This disaster (or perhaps I should call it a near disaster, since no one was killed) occurred on my fourth trip on the Rio Grande de Santiago. It was the closest call I've ever had.

The Mexican engineers had by that time completed two dams on the Rio Grande de Santiago, but it still left us some exciting rapids if we started below the second dam.

I had by this time begun to gain a national reputation, yet for some reason I still had a hard time scraping up more than nine or ten people for the Mexican expeditions. I also always had more men than women who wanted to go on the Mexican trips. Women would gladly go to Canada or Alaska, but for some reason, not to Mexico. Although I encouraged as many

people as possible to join me, because of a few unexpected problems (such as we encountered on this fourth Rio Grande de Santiago trip) I now limit my Mexican trips mostly to boatmen who've been on the Colorado with me for years and who can take anything a river can throw at them.

I had run the Rio Grande de Santiago three times, and the last time I made it look so easy that I decided, with a little encouragement from Orville, to talk this trip up as a milk run. As a result, when I left the United States I had a party of two men: Orville, who goes on all the Mexican trips; and Dr. Bob Baer, a Northern California physician who had run the Colorado with me several times before; and six women (Bimbo, Bob Baer's wife Ann; Lee, a Chicago pediatrician; Kay and Barbara, San Jose, California nurses; Kim, a young woman from Detroit; and Ann, a New York secretary who replaced one of my regulars at the last minute.)

We arrived in Guadalajara August 26, took our usual air reconnaissance, then hired a truck for the trip to the river. I always run these Mexican rivers at about the same time every year, since this is the middle of the Mexican rainy season and the water is high then. The only drawback is that Mexican rains are more like cloudbursts than rain. The heavens just open up and pour, and no matter what kind of rain clothes we're wearing, we always get soaked clear through to the skin.

Often so much water comes down at one time, it just stands on the streets, roadways, and other paved surfaces unable to run off fast enough. Frequently in August and September the Guadalajara

Airport resembles a huge shallow lake, and when our plane lands it throws up huge plumes of water on either side. Sometimes, too, during the rainy season, huge quantities of water rush down the rivers, causing them to overflow their banks and flood hundreds of square miles of Mexican countryside, wiping out roads, bridges, farms and often entire villages.

This is a terrible time of the year to travel in Mexico and I guess I've spent more time huddling miserably in the back of a truck in the driving rain than I care to remember. For a white water river runner like I am, though, it's also the only season to travel there. I don't care for the driving rain, but the rest of the year Mexico is extremely dry and the water level drops drastically, exposing hundreds of sandbars and making raft travel almost impossible. Given a choice, I'd rather brave a little rain and the huge waters of the flood stage rivers than have to push those heavy rafts off the sandbars during low water.

This trip to the river was even rougher than usual. We piled in back of the truck under the canvas but the driving rain went right through, soaking us to the skin almost immediately. Several of the girls began to shake uncontrollably so we huddled together as close as possible in a futile attempt to keep warm. To complicate matters we also had to keep absolutely quiet as we passed the checkpoints since the driver had warned us that it was illegal for him to haul passengers in back. The military road to the dam was steep, narrow, winding, and typical of Mexico. Here and there rocks rumbled down the steep hillside and bounced across the road. At one point a rock slide blocked our path, forcing us to scramble out and throw rocks off the road. Under these conditions I guess I shouldn't have been surprised when, on reaching our destination, the driver jumped out, tossed off our boats and other gear, and roared off with the words, "Got to get back."

I just stood there, dumbfounded, as I watched the truck tail lights disappear up the mountain road. Later I heard he had just barely made it out before a huge rock slide cut off the road for several days.

We stood there for a few minutes with the water running down inside our rain clothes, then suddenly we realized the river had started to rise and threatened to carry off the gear. Everybody sprang into action then and we spent the next couple of hours miserably dragging the heavy boats, motors, and other equipment up the slopes to safety. After that we faced the gloomy prospect of crawling into our sleeping bags in the driving rain or trying to put up the tents in what were by now almost gale-force winds.

"I'll be darned if I'm going to bed in those wet sleeping bags," one of the girls said at that point. "I'm going to dry out in that Cantina I saw up there by the dam." That sounded pretty good to all of us so we headed in that direction. The Mexican owner was delighted to see us and kept serving *cervesa* as long as we'd buy. Finally about three in the morning we could hold no more, so we headed back to some very wet sleeping bags.

We woke a few hours later to a beautiful sunny morning. The water was now coming out of the dam gates full blast—

The Rio Grande de Santiago has forced people to come up with a lot of ingenious ways of getting things across.

higher than anything I'd seen on the Colorado. A short time later the superintendent came down to discuss the situation. He definitely didn't want us to go. But Orville talked to him and after a few minutes he said he would shut down the gates soon, then we could go in safety. So I got the pumps and began to blow up the boats by hand. Before they were completely inflated, I heard a shout and looked up to see a Mexican running downhill from the dam. When he reached the boats he started untieing the lines, threw them in the boats violently and said in English, "Go, now!"

That startled us so much we piled in and shoved off immediately without knowing what was happening. The minute we got in the water I worked frantically to get the motor started because just a short distance away was one whale of a rapid. The motor sputtered, sputtered again, then burst into life with a roar. My plan was to miss the first rocks, then keep near shore for the rest of the way. I cleared the big rock, then gave the motor full power.

Instead of spurting across to safety as I intended, the half-inflated raft simply doubled under with the added power. A huge wave caught us and suddenly swept us into the biggest hole I'd ever seen, bouncing us every which way. The upstream boat pitched upward sharply, then turned over the middle one, throwing Barbara out into the churning water. We grabbed her as she went by and pulled her back into the raft.

Now the water had started to slow down a little, and using partial power to keep the boats from doubling up again, I managed to reach the bank and grab some trees. I didn't dare tie up, though, because we had pulled in under heavy overhanging branches and if the water came back up we'd find ourselves trapped. Although we hadn't traveled very far down the river I decided to spend the rest of the day and night here so I could finish pumping and untangling the boats. We slept on the boats that night, and next morning the water had dropped almost ten feet, enough to give us fifteen or twenty feet of beach on which to bring up the boats. I managed to inflate all rafts in a few hours and just before noon we were ready to launch again.

On all Mexican trips, of course, everyone knows about the alligators and crocodiles, but once on the water I usually keep quiet about them. Somehow just the reminder seems to make people nervous and prone to mistakes. This trip especially had started badly and those inexperienced young women had become extremely apprehensive about the rest of the trip. For this reason I told Orville not to play up the idea that we'd be seeing alligators along the river.

Next morning the entire mood changed and the girls were now good-naturedly cracking jokes with one another. I was glad to see that the trip had finally begun to settle down. For the next few hours things went well and Orville settled back into his normal pattern of teasing the girls as we went along. We shot through a number of interesting rapids, then about noon I began to notice a few long stringy plants in the current.

Later I learned that these plants grow in the lake above the dam and when you see them in the river downstream it means the flood gates are open. At that point, however, the appearance of these plants in the river meant nothing to me.

The water had now begun to pick up speed. I'm not sure why I failed to notice what was happening, but I didn't sense the danger until suddenly I realized we were going faster and faster—then I heard an ominous roar like a runaway freight train. I knew immediately what that meant. Huge boulders were being rolled along the bottom of the river by the gigantic water.

Then it hit me. The Mexican engineers had turned the entire dam loose above us and here we were caught in the middle. The motor whirred, then sprang to life. I gunned it frantically trying to swing into shore. I could have saved the effort. It was like trying to push a feather against a hurricane. I glanced frantically downriver.

A half mile ahead the river made a sharp, right angle turn and headed off in another direction.

We'd never make it. "Hang on!" I shouted. "No matter what, hang onto the boats." It was the safest thing to do. Even if a raft turns upside down you can live quite awhile on the air trapped between the bottom of the boat and the water.

We were starting around now, carried along by the rushing water. Then everything went crazy. The first boat tipped straight up, the middle boat disappeared under water, and the end boat flipped upright, hung precariously, then slapped down on top of the others. Suddenly I was hanging on the side. In a few minutes, Bob and Ann floated by. That low in the water I couldn't see anybody else. For all I knew the others had been swept into the water and drowned. We now swung around a bend so close to the bank that I knew we could make it to shore. It's funny how people react in situations like this. I have always become completely calm in the face of disaster. That's exactly what happened in this case. My mind methodically clicked off the possibilities.

I knew that the trip was now over and my primary responsibility was to get the group out safely. I had to act.

"Take Ann and hike to the highway," I shouted at Bob. "When you reach Guadalajara get a plane. I'll hike the group out."

That sounds like a mouthful to blurt out when you're shooting along in the water, but I had to make up my mind fast because I probably wouldn't get another chance. In addition we had come into a slight backwater and I had a few seconds in which to make a decision.

Bob looked at me for a minute, then nodded, "Okay, Boss Lady."

He then headed for shore, taking Ann with him. At this point I thought Bob understood I wanted him to hike out. I found out later he simply thought I wanted him to get ashore. I watched while he and Ann climbed out on shore. I was shooting along in the current again hanging onto the boat. Then it caught a wave and shot out of sight before I could grab it. For a minute I could see the other rafts about one thousand yards ahead with Orville and the girls hanging on. Orville wasn't moving. That's not like him. I knew I must reach them. Suddenly I gasped. It had just hit me, we were now almost to the thirty-foot-high dam that we almost catapulted over on the first Mexican trip. If they dropped over that dam, I'd probably lose every one of them.

Because of my early freelance swims in the high water of the Colorado I had little fear. I knew from past experience that if you put your feet down in a life jacket in the current you'd hit the fastest part of the water and take off like lightning, but if you bring your feet up and put your arms around your knees you'll just bump along from side to side.

I put my feet down then and really took off. That swim was something. At first it was hard to tell that I was making any headway. Then I could see I was coming closer. After that I began to close the gap fast. It took all my knowledge to catch that boat because we were going through a lot of large rapids as well as some fairly fast water. In those, I just leaned back with my knees up and got through somehow.

Once again I sighted the boat. Everyone

was hanging on for dear life. I was coming closer and closer. Finally I lunged and barely caught the line with my fingertips.

"Orville," I yelled at the top of my lungs, "what's wrong?"

He turned toward me with glazed eyes, stared at me for a minute, then said, "You're the best-looking thing I've ever seen."

I screamed again, "Orville, what the hell are you doing in the water? Why aren't you up there on the raft getting those girls out? You'll never get to shore with all that weight hanging straight down—Orville, we're almost on top of the dam."

"Get your breath," I shouted. "I'm going to jump on your shoulders—give me the bow line."

Orville looked at me sheepishly. "I can't. It's caught in the buckle of my life preserver."

"Oh for heaven sakes, Orville," I said. "Go to work on it."

I then jumped on top of the raft and began to pull the others up. "Watch your chance," I told everybody. "Grab a tree if you can, then go to land."

Suddenly I heard a voice directly underneath us below the boat. "Oh my God, who was that?"

"My life preserver's caught," the voice gasped. "I'm trapped."

"It's just a little nylon string," I said. "Turn your hands loose and we'll watch for you on all sides."

In a minute Lee, the pediatrician, bobbed up, and a dozen hands grabbed her and pulled the sobbing woman on top with the rest of us. At this point the raft hit a cross current and swung sharply into the bank. I grabbed the branch of a tree with the line in my hand, jumped to shore, and brought the boats in.

Once I got everybody on shore I took a headcount. Kim, the girl from Detroit, was missing. Was she lost in the jungle? Had she been swept downriver? Was she dead? I didn't know. I'd have to make a decision about her shortly. I also told Bimbo Baer that I had sent Bob for help. That upset her more than I expected. The experience apparently had left her quite shaken. I now turned to the physical problems. I pulled all boats out on shore and found the food and sleeping bags still there and in good shape. The boats themselves were twisted but they looked beautiful. I had some decisions to make so Orville and I walked a few feet away and talked it over. The others seemed in bad emotional condition. If we continued on the river we would have to carry the boats and equipment around the mine dam, now less than a mile away. I didn't think the girls could handle it in the shape they were in. That's when I made up my mind for sure that I would abandon my boats right there on the river. That hurt because they would cost several thousand dollars to replace. I had, of course, made this decision tentatively when I sent Bob Baer out for a plane. But even then I somehow hoped that I could salvage something. I couldn't and I faced it right there.

That behind me, I turned to the other problems. I had been eyeing the cliffs along the river for some time and believed I could hike the girls out over them. Somewhere beyond I knew we'd find a usable airstrip. And if Bob and Ann made it, we'd also find an airplane waiting. I also made a decision about Kim. I decided we couldn't do much searching in the jungle now. We'd stay right where we were that night. Then next day we'd hike along the river and see what we found.

Next morning we started off through the thick jungle along the river bank.

A short time later Orville and I stopped to talk under a tree when I glanced up to see Bob and Ann across the river walking hypnotically toward the mine dam. I saw that they hadn't understood that they were supposed to go for a plane.

Even though they looked across a couple of times, they just ignored us and pushed on downriver.

"Halt," Orville shouted in that big voice of his. That seemed to break the spell and they stopped.

Orville and I now held a hurried conference. It was still a good idea, we decided, for them to hike out over the ridge and bring an airplane. After shouting back and forth across the roar of the water, they nodded their agreement. Then as I watched, they disappeared into the jungle. After we started on upriver again, I noticed the girls weren't talking much. They were also hiking quite slowly. I didn't realize, however, that anything was wrong until one of the girls let out a terrified scream and started sobbing uncontrollably. Her sleeping bag caught on a branch and she simply went all to pieces. It was then that I realized all of them were on the verge of panic.

"Orville," I said, "I can't take the girls up that cliff. In their condition I'd kill at least one of them. We'll just have to cross the river and hike out over those rolling hills on the other side."

He looked at me strangely for a mo-

This is what rivers look like during flood season as they near the ocean in Mexico, and spread out over fields and farms near Santiago Ixquintla.

ment, then said, "Georgie I'm not sure we'll get any of them to go back in the water." That left me with a problem.

About that time I heard a yell on the other side of the river. There was movement on the bank. It was our missing Kim. She had dislocated her shoulder in the river and one arm hung limp by her side. In sign language we made her understand that she should sit tight and we'd come to her. That relieved me. Everyone was accounted for. I had another conference with Orville. Then I walked over to where the girls were sprawled on the ground and broke the news. "Oh no," they sobbed. "We can't." Then they broke down and bawled.

I knew we'd have to do something, so Orville and I started working on them. Orville would pet them, then I'd bawl them out. "You've got food and water," I told them, "what more do you want?"

Long ago I discovered that this is an excellent technique for bringing people back to their senses. It shocks them into seeing things as they really are.

By next morning everyone had agreed to try crossing. I then put a rope through the bags to keep them together and we started pushing bags in front of us across the river. We simply picked a narrow spot and waded in. The current was fast and strong and carried us for some distance before we could climb out on the bank. Within a short time, however, we had all made it across without difficulty and with instructions from the pediatrician, Orville managed to put Kim's shoulder back in place.

That was one major obstacle behind us. Now we had to tackle the jungle and the hills beyond. Unlike farmers in the United States, Mexican farmers plant their cornfields high on the hills. I've seen Mexican cornfields near the top of some very high mountains and on some of the steepest slopes imaginable. For that reason, I knew that somewhere beyond those near hills we'd find cornfields, beyond that a village, and hopefully, nearby, an airstrip.

The jungle along the river was extremely thick and the going very difficult as we started out. I also knew that poisonous snakes lived in the jungle around us so I picked up a large stick and began to wave it back and forth in front of me.

"What are you doing, Georgie?" one of the girls asked in a frightened voice.

"I'm just the nervous type," I told her. "I have to keep active all the time." I didn't dare tell her the truth.

Generally, however, the girls were making it through the jungle without too much difficulty. The exception to this was Kim. I always insist that my trip members wear tennis shoes, but against my better judgement I had allowed Kim to come on the trip. She was a complete greenhorn who knew absolutely nothing about wilderness travel. When she showed up ready to go, she had brought along only one pair of suede shoes. I should have turned her back right there, but I didn't realize that was the only pair she had brought until much too late. Once wet, those shoes shrank until they became completely unbearable. Every step was difficult and painful. Finally I made her stop and cut the toes out. This gave some relief, but exposed her feet to bruising from sticks and rocks on the ground.

At the top of the first hill we spotted not only cornfields, but a hut with a few chickens and dogs nearby. I couldn't see anyone there, but I knew there would at least be a trail that would lead to a nearby village. Generally the back-country Mexicans use the village system with the cornfields located in a rough circle around them. The Mexican farmers work these fields during the day, then return to the villages at night.

Just as we reached the edge of the first field one of the girls spotted a rattler. She was horrified, but I felt relieved. Those poisonous Mexican snakes rather horrify me, but the rattler seems rather friendly and old hat since I've run into them many times along the Colorado. There I never let anyone touch the snakes since I consider them an essential part of nature.

At the hut we found two trails going

This is the rugged terrain that we had to hike through when we were forced to abandon the rafts on that third Mexican trip.

in different directions. Orville and I discussed what to do, then finally decided to take the right fork and see if it ended in the village. It looked well traveled so we started out with high hopes. The trail ran along the ridge for awhile, then began to climb upwards. At the edge of a far cornfield it simply ran out. This often happens since many of the trails simply connect outlying fields from a central point. There across a steep valley we could see the other trail wandering along a far ridge.

"Let's cut across," one of the girls said. "It's much too far back."

"No way," I told her. "In your condition you'd never make it. We'll go back down this trail to the hut and up the other branch. It may be farther, but that brush down there in the gully is pretty rough going."

It had begun to get dark now so we made a makeshift camp and settled down to spend the night. Next morning the fog had rolled in and visibility was poor. The trail was quite plain so we picked up our gear and headed back down. Suddenly from below a group of hostile looking Mexican men came out of the brush and started up the slope.

"This is it," I thought to myself. "I've finally run up against those famous Mexican *bandidos*. The nearest man regarded me sternly, then suddenly broke into a broad grin. These were cornfield guards. Seeing us on the other trail they assumed *we* were bandits. But once they saw the women, they knew we had to be Americans. Mexican women don't usually travel with the men in the bush like this. Now they greeted us happily, talking all at once.

Kim's feet, at this point, were in ter-

rible shape and I couldn't see how she could walk much farther, so I showed the bleeding feet to the Mexican in charge. A short time later one of them showed up with a burro for Kim to ride. The other men also picked up some of our packs and started off toward the village. A short time before we reached the village itself a plane came winging over the nearby hills, circled the village a couple of times and sat down on the new airstrip built that year by the village school children.

The occupants, we discovered a short time later, were Bob Baer and Ann, come to fly us out to Guadalajara. Everything seemed to come together simply and easily in the end, but it really wasn't that way at all. Although the plane came in as if on cue, getting to that point for Bob and Ann was almost as eventful an experience as our own.

When Bob and Ann reached shore they regained their bearings and immediately began to go through two black neoprene bags they had grabbed in the river for flotation. By one of those weird coincidences those bags turned out to be the key to our eventual rescue.

The river had sucked off Ann's shoes, and the bags contained a pair of sneakers which fit her. They also contained a camera, one sleeping bag, an air mattress, some pesos, a few U.S. dollars and $300 in traveler's checks. (The bag belonged to Lee, our Chicago pediatrician.) At this point I naturally assumed they were on their way out for help. As it turned out, they hadn't understood a word I had said. As I've discovered, sometimes when people are under stress, nothing much registers.

After we had our shouting match

across the river however and they understood what I wanted they headed out across the steep ridges in earnest, and a day later crossed a pass almost three thousand feet above the river. There on the other side lay still another range.

Suddenly in the distance, Bob saw a figure. There it was again. Together they began to shout *"Succoro!* Help! *Succoro!"* Within a short time a barefoot Mexican worked his way across the ridge and Ann began to explain their problem in Spanish.

Since they had not eaten for almost two days, the Mexican (his name was Pedro) first took them several miles to some tomales he had stashed in a tree. Then after they had eaten he led them back to the Village of Cinco Minas. Here once a week a truck brought supplies from another back-country village. From there they could catch a bus to Guadalajara.

When they reached Cinco Minas, the truck was there and left within the hour. They caught it. At the next village, however, all the buses to Guadalajara were full.

Not to be stopped, Bob found an old black limousine in the village and rented it. Then with a Mexican driver at the wheel they roared at top speed into Guadalajara.

Once in the city they rented a small plane (Ann was by then becoming an expert at forging Lee's signature on the traveler's checks) and they began to search all the airstrips our party could possibly hike to.

At one point they flew directly over us. We waved and tried to flash them with a silver tarp, but they just couldn't see us.

After trying a couple of small villages, they landed at Salo Mita and talked to the local school teacher.

"The village guards," he told them, "are bringing in some *bandidos* now; one of them is a blonde lady."

That had to be Kay. We were the *bandidos*. Bob then crawled back in the plane, flew out for some beer and came back. An hour later we trudged into Salo Mita with our escort. What a tearful scene! Everyone tried to hug Bob and Ann at once. Bimbo and Bob embraced tearfully. The party was now back together again.

An hour later the plane ferried us to Guadalajara in two separate groups and a short time later we found ourselves together again in a Guadalajara hotel.

While everything turned out all right except for my having to leave my boats, I'm afraid I lost a few river rats on that trip. None of the girls ever went near white water again. The nurses who had sworn to remain single the rest of their lives, promptly returned home and got married. And Dr. Baer's wife lost all interest in ever running a river again.

I'm not quite sure why, but this reaction startled and disappointed me. I guess I love river exploration so much that I'll take anything a river will throw me and come back for more. For this reason, I'm surprised when other people don't react the same way.

Despite problems like these that I've occasionally run into in Mexican waters, I've always enjoyed the area and the experience. During my years of exploring rivers in Mexico, I managed at one time to join a Mexican mountain climbing club. Sometimes when I would fly to Mexico for a river trip, I would also try to climb one of their mountains. On one trip, I climbed

I always loved the warmth and camaraderie of the people we met on the trips into Mexico. We had some wonderful times.

Popocatepetl. My most memorable experience, however, occurred on a nearby seventeen-thousand-foot peak.

Orville and I had flown into Mexico City several days before, and we decided to join the climbing club for a hike scheduled to leave at two o'clock the next morning. That night, the Mexicans gave a tremendous party with music, drinking, and dancing. It looked like fun but Orville and I decided that we had better go to bed early and wake up fresh for the next day's hike. Two a.m. came and we climbed on the bus. I'm not the nervous type but that was the worst bus ride that I have ever taken. That driver veered out over the cliffs, almost crashed head-on several times, and passed blind around curves at top speed. I gripped the back of the seat in front of me and hung on for dear life. The Mexicans however, who had stayed up late, were now snoring in their seats.

Finally we stopped. When I climbed off that bus I was exhausted. The Mexicans however, fresh from their recent sleep, laughed and joked and got ready to climb the mountain.

I dragged all the way up that peak. At one point someone started passing around a bottle. I thought they were drinking mountain sickness medicine. It turned out to be red wine. At the top, someone strummed on a guifar, everyone cheered and the hiker in front of me gave me a kiss and a hug. They indicated I had to hug the hiker coming up below me. I loved it. The Mexican mountains aren't all that interesting to me, but the camaraderie really turns me on.

*   *   *

The only real fly in the ointment I have ever found in Mexico is the country's customs officials. That experience always leaves a bad taste in my mouth. I don't mind paying legitimate government fees but I do object to individual bribes.

In the beginning, I'd simply pay the first worker I came to, then when I got to the next one I'd pay again. Sometimes I paid five or six times before I received final clearance. Then I discovered that if I went right to the top immediately and received the proper stamp, nobody bothered me again. Of course, no one actually asks for a bribe. They always hide it as a part of the legitimate tariff, but I always wind up paying a lot more than I'm actually suppose to.

I've discovered too, that if I am in a real hurry, I might as well forget it. Official machinery in Mexico not only grinds slowly, but it's also very formal and gracious. I can't simply pay my money, pick up my equipment and go. I always had to sit down and have a drink and make polite, formal chit-chat. I'm a pretty impatient, informal person and I'd much prefer to spend this time on the river.

Generally I don't have much trouble getting through customs with my boats, but the rules of the game change constantly. This always means more lost time. Several years ago, for instance, I arrived in Guadalajara ready to go and discovered I couldn't pick up my boats at the airport as I generally do, but had to claim them somewhere else in the city. Orville and I drove to the address we were given which turned out to be a huge warehouse. I'd never seen anything like it. That warehouse contained dozens of American cars, motorcycles, and almost everything else imaginable. After awhile one of the workers came over to see what we wanted. When we told him he immediately asked for money.

"Let's go Orville," I said. "If I pay him I'll just have to pay half-a-dozen other workers before I get out of here. Let's go back to customs and start there." So back we went. We saw the top man and after the usual amenities, received the proper papers. Next day back at the warehouse we claimed our boats with no trouble at all.

On another trip, instead of running a river entirely within the boundaries of Mexico I decided to start on the Balsas in Guatamala and finish several hundred miles downstream in Mexico. As usual I didn't consider the complications. I simply applied for and received visas for both countries, then began the trip.

I came downriver, entered Mexico, pulled the boats out and stored them in a Mexico City warehouse to await our next trip. I had done something similar to this several times before so I didn't think very much of it. Then, since everyone else had decided to stay and explore Mexico, I headed for the airport by myself to board my plane back to Los Angeles. The Mexican official I handed my passport to, took one look and disappeared for about ten minutes. He then came back, asked a couple of questions, and disappeared again.

"Oh, oh," I said to myself. "There's something wrong here."

Finally he came back again and said that the chief custom official wanted to see me. With that I knew I had a real problem.

When I reached the office we went through all the amenities again: drinks; lunch; polite conversation. Finally the official said, "Señora, we have no record of you ever entering Mexico."

So that was the problem. Since I entered Mexico on the river I hadn't gone through any of their checkpoints. As far as I was concerned it all seemed pretty simple to explain, but the more I talked the more confused he became.

Finally I wound up with a whole room full of officials trying to understand what had happened. And although several officials spoke excellent English, no one could believe that I had come from Guatamala down a river on a raft. Eventually they all shook their heads and told me I shouldn't leave the office until I could board my plane. As near as I could figure they decided that someone in their office had made a mistake and if they could rush me out before a higher-up discovered the problem, they wouldn't have any trouble.

When my plane landed they put me in a jeep with an armed guard and whizzed me out to the runway to make sure that I got on board first. When the other Americans came aboard some twenty minutes later they all wanted to know how I rated such special treatment. I'm not quite sure I ever really figured that out.

I can see how it might be difficult to understand the travels of a woman river runner, but to completely close your mind to the fact that people can and do, do such things is, to me, mind-blowing. I'm afraid that no matter how long I continue to explore Mexico, I'll just never understand the workings of the Mexican bureaucracy.

When I first started exploring the country I had in mind running many of the South American rivers as well. One experience, however, convinced me that South America was not for me. During the summer of 1966 I decided to try several rivers in Ecuador and Peru:

The Rio Napa, which turned out to be big and placid with lots of campsites; Rio Maranon through the Andes, with lots of rapids; and the Pongo de Manseriche, with its whirlpools and cascades.

If I thought Mexican officials were tied up in red tape, the South American countries were many times worse. The main problem is that you are dealing with two foreign countries and you need permits from both governments, including the army. That means a great deal of socializing. If you have the time and money,

that's fine, but since you go from one army's control to another, negotiations can become quite sticky. When I started to run the South American rivers I ran into an American colonel in Peru who was delighted to see me but who warned me of the problem. "You're small," he told me. "You have very little influence, and you could easily wind up without your boats."

There are other problems: the Indians in the area still shoot and kill people each year and we were warned not to land in their territory. In addition, the American missionaries there are quite unfriendly. The reason, I feel, is that they live very high and they don't want anyone knowing too much about their affairs. Some, I observed, owned fancy cars, their own airplanes, huge houses and more. They made it very clear to me that they certainly didn't want us nosing around.

The fact is that while the rivers there are fairly interesting to run, the whole atmosphere surrounding the trip is unfriendly, and a river trip should be a friendly, joyous affair. When I compare the reception I received in South America to the warm welcome I always get from the natives in Mexico, I realize that I just don't need the hassle. As a result I vowed several years ago not to explore South America again—at least not until a number of changes take place.

I have, from time to time, spent a number of hours in the air over Central and South America looking for rivers to explore. I've flown extensively over the Amazon and a number of other South American rivers. The problem with streams coming out of the Andes, is that they are too steep at the upper end, with cascading waterfalls, and too calm after they leave the mountains. Very few have that special quality that makes them good white-water rivers.

I still intend to explore the rivers of Mexico for a number of years to come. The rivers themselves are a challenge and the people are always a delight. As I mentioned before the great sense of well-being received from running a wilderness river is really what these white-water trips are all about. As long as I can enjoy my river adventures in a congenial atmosphere, then I'm ready to go back again and again.

Epilogue

It is Monday, June 10. The temperature here at Lee's Ferry, Arizona, has already hit 110 degrees in the shade. I don't ordinarily mind the heat, but I have been working on these boats in the hot broiling sun for the last five hours and I'm tired of it.

I put down the beer I've been drinking and look out at the river. It is running clear, cold and sparkling today at about 6000 cubic feet per second. That's not like the old days when I used to leave here on the huge 125,000 cubic-feet-a-second water, but it's enough volume to make all the rapids interesting.

I have already run one trip through the Grand Canyon this season; now I'm about ready to leave on the second. Several boatmen and I spent most of yesterday and all of this morning unloading the boats, blowing them up and lashing them together. Now five boats sit on the edge of the Colorado River waiting for their passengers who will be here momentarily.

I've been through all this before, of course, but somehow I never get tired of it. Every time I run the rapids there are different people, different situations, and different challengers.

Orville has already indicated to me that he's in rare form for this trip.

"I've got a new topless idea for you," he told me awhile ago. "I'll unfold it as we go along."

"Don't bother," I said. "I'm not about to go topless again."

Actually he doesn't know it, but I'm about to put him in his place again. I know Orville likes to tease the girls, and the worst thing I can do is to isolate him from the women. So I plan to load his boat with men only. I can hear the moans now. But then I can't let Orville think he's the only one who can play practical jokes. Now two buses have turned off the main highway and are headed directly toward me. The brakes squeal—my new passengers have arrived. There are eighty of them and they are from all over the United States. Actually I only take forty people with me, the other forty go in a different group headed by Don Scutchfield and Ron Huff. The Park Service wants groups kept fairly small.

The bus door opens. Bob Olsen, one of my boatmen, struts off wearing ragged cut-off jeans and singing "Proud Mary" at the top of his voice. "Ballin' . . . Ballin' . . . Ballin' on the river." Bob always makes up his own version.

Plop! An orange hits him in the back of the head. I can see the boatmen are going to be in rare form this trip. But then there are other times and places to be serious; the river was meant for fun. Another boatman comes off and lets out a war whoop.

Now the passengers: a middle-aged woman from Detroit comes first wearing neat green slacks and a big floppy hat. I can guarantee she won't look that neat after I've run her through the rapids a few times. A family comes down the steps: mother; father; and two boys about seven and eight. They'll have a ball. A stoop-shouldered man in his early seventies steps off next. His family wrote wondering if he should come. I talked to him on the phone and then told them not to worry. When they meet him at Las Vegas at the end of the trip they won't recognize him.

Finally the neoprene bags are piled in front of the boats and thirty minutes later I push off downriver with twenty eager life-jacketed people aboard.

We pull through the first ripple just below Lee's Ferry, the boat rocks a few times and a couple of cold waves wash over the passengers. I can still remember running this ripple for the movie "Six Girls Against the Colorado," over and over. Did I get bored!

"What was that rapid?" a woman asks me.

"That's no rapid, that's just a *miscellaneous*," I tell her.

Mile 6: Everyone looks up as we pass under Navajo Bridge. U.S. 89 crosses Marble Canyon here. The bridge looks a mile high but it's only 467 feet above the river. It's our last trace of civilization until we pass Phantom Ranch, the third day out.

Now Mile 8 and Badger Creek, the first rapid on the river. I came in on the tongue, the front end of the boat tips up, the motor roars, a wave washes the length of the raft, someone screams. We are on our way.

"We hit the really big ones the third day," I tell them. "Just wait."

And so I am off down the Grand Canyon again doing what I love best, for I am Georgie Clark, Woman of the River and if I have my way, I shall repeat these trips through the biggest rapids in the world, over and over and over again . . . forever!